MEDITATIONS FOR ADVENT
AND CHRISTMAS

Books by James G. Kirk

Meditations for Advent and Christmas

Meditations for Lent

When We Gather:
A Book of Prayers for Worship
Year A   Year B   Year C

MEDITATIONS FOR ADVENT AND CHRISTMAS

JAMES G. KIRK

Westminster/John Knox Press
Louisville, Kentucky

Unless otherwise identified, scripture quotations are from the Revised Standard Version of the Bible, copyrighted 1946, 1952, © 1971, 1973 by the Division of Christian Education of the National Council of the Churches of Christ in the U.S.A., and are used by permission.

The quotation marked NEB is from *The New English Bible.* © The Delegates of the Oxford University Press and the Syndics of the Cambridge University Press 1961, 1970. Used by permission.

Portions of the Foreword appeared in slightly different form in *Journal for Preachers* (vol. 10, no. 1) under the title "Prayers for the People."

Woodcuts by Virgil Solis, 1562. Reproduced from *Luther's Meditations on the Gospels.* Translated and Arranged by Roland H. Bainton. Copyright © MCMLXII W. L. Jenkins. Published by The Westminster Press.

Book design by Gene Harris

First edition

Published by Westminster/John Knox Press
Louisville, Kentucky

PRINTED IN THE UNITED STATES OF AMERICA
9 8 7 6 5 4 3 2 1

Library of Congress Cataloging-in-Publication Data

Kirk, James G.
    Meditations for Advent and Christmas / James G. Kirk. — 1st ed.
       p.   cm.
    Includes bibliographical references and index.
    ISBN 0-664-25057-2

    1. Advent—Meditations. 2. Christmas—Meditations. I. Title.
BV40.K56 1989
242'.33—dc19
                                  88-39659
                                    CIP

To my wife,
Elizabeth J.,
a constant source
of companionship,
inspiration,
and joy

CONTENTS

FOREWORD

The dominant themes for the seasons of Advent and Christmas are watchfulness, promise, preparation, fulfillment, and celebration. We hear in scripture how we are to watch at all times for the day that will come. It will be a day of great glory. The valleys shall be filled, mountains and hills made low, the crooked shall be made straight, and the rough places smooth.

First, a time of watchfulness. We are told to wait for the messenger's coming and give thanks for his righteousness by which we are saved from wrath. He will walk with us in the valleys of sorrow. He can level the barriers we erect to evade his will. His paths are straight; we need only to follow. God's mercy allows us to watch for the day of the messenger's coming, and for that we give thanks.

Second, we receive a promise. The promise is of Emmanuel, God with us. What a glorious gift! The words of the prophet are fulfilled in the birth of a child. What is conceived of the Holy Spirit and carried in Mary's womb is the promise of eternal life to all who believe. Jesus will save God's people from their signs, and God will dwell in their midst.

That is why the headings of the meditations in this book are verbs instead of nouns. Verbs are appropriate to the season. God took the initiative to get personally involved in history. No longer could anyone accuse God of being aloof, apart, remote, or distant. Here was Emmanuel about to be born; Jesus, the child of Mary.

Through the power of the Holy Spirit, this Holy One reveals forevermore the depth of God's wisdom and the wonder of God's salvation. As we commit our lives to Christ and learn of his will, we give thanks for God's manifold gifts, which embrace all of life.

Third, Advent is a time for preparation. The people are to be ready. John comes, crying in the wilderness, "Prepare the way of the Lord, make his paths straight" (Mark 1:3). There shall be baptism with water; Jesus will baptize with the Holy Spirit. There shall be confession of sins; Jesus will be the means of repentance.

Advent marks a fresh beginning as we hear anew of the redemption the Messiah brings. When we are tempted to waver, we know that we need to step out with confidence. When we are alone, we need the comfort God's Spirit brings. When we hurt, we seek the healing touch of the great Physician to ease our pain. When we are confused, we seek once again the reassuring words, "Behold, the days are coming [when] I will cause a righteous Branch to spring forth who shall execute justice and righteousness in the land" (Jer. 33:14-15). We prepare ourselves to receive the one who reveals that righteousness, Jesus the Christ.

A fourth theme of Advent is fulfillment. John sends his disciples to find out if Jesus is the awaited Messiah. Jesus tells them to report what they have seen and heard: The blind see, the deaf hear, lepers are cleansed, the poor hear good news, the dead are raised. When John's disciples leave, Jesus tells the crowd John's identity; "more than a prophet," he is the one divinely sent to prepare the way for God's reign. The signs of that reign are already present in the midst of God's people.

We are the heirs of that reign, the sons and daughters of righteousness and children of the covenant. By God's grace we bear the name "Christian" and are members of Christ's household of faith. The meditations reveal the responsibility we have for one another and how closely we are bound together as the family of faith.

Celebration is the fifth theme of Advent and Christmas. As shepherds watched their flocks, God's glory shone on them. They heard the angel say, "Be not afraid." A star would guide them to where a birth had occurred. Full of joy, they would behold an event that promised peace on earth. Today, followers still gather to celebrate what happened: God brought forth Jesus, whose cause was righteousness. The everlasting response has been to rejoice and be glad.

The carols we sing tell of God's glory, how angels sang and shepherds watched as a star led them to behold such wonder. With the amazement and wonder of Christ's revelation, we celebrate the many ways the Holy Spirit surprises us and visits us and causes us to feel Christ's presence. As at the marriage at Cana, Christ is found in the laughter and gaiety of noisy gatherings. On solemn occasions Christ's majesty and strength evoke awe and praise.

Throughout, the meditations seek to proclaim God's word as we await and then celebrate the day of the messenger's coming. It is a day that brings the righteousness which saves God's people from wrath. God has come as a child born of Mary, full of promise and grace. Through the Holy Spirit, Emmanuel reveals forevermore God's wisdom and the wonder of God's salvation. We can now be called heirs of God's righteousness and children of the covenant.

The meditations seek to remind us of how God's faithfulness accompanies us through the valleys of life. Barriers are leveled and paths become straight.

It is a faithfulness that endures from age to age and is grounded in incomparable wisdom. It embraces the believer in ultimate salvation. Such faithfulness will no doubt surprise us, since God has a way of interrupting humanity's agenda and revealing God in unexpected ways. Christ is called on to intercede with compassion, providing mercy to endure the day of his coming, the refining sacrifice that cleanses tarnished souls and purifies thoughts, and the empowerment of the Holy Spirit which enables us to respond.

Our response then is to greater commitment, to step out with confidence in spite of risks. Such confidence will be bred of God's grace and mercy, involve learning Christ's will for our lives, submitting those lives to the guidance of God's Holy Spirit, executing justice and righteousness throughout the land, and standing before God's judgment seat in awe and eternal praise.

These meditations are a tribute to those who have made and will make that commitment. They are sent forth in the hope that they will provide guidance and inspiration as we make our pilgrimage day by day, help us to behold the wondrous deeds God has wrought through the ages, and reaffirm by God's grace our intention to go and see this wondrous thing that has come to pass.

Throughout the meditations you will notice that the scriptures used rehearse as well as anticipate. Advent has that double significance: It lets you look backward as well as forward. Looking backward, you rehearse how God has been faithful during the entire course of salvation history. Looking forward, you anticipate that God will continue to fulfill what God has promised.

Some of the scriptures I chose are those recommended by the Supplemental Liturgical Resource

Daily Prayer (Westminster Press, 1987). Others I chose in order to provide this backward-forward glimpse, hoping to keep in tension that which is to come based upon what has already occurred. It is not until after the Fourth Sunday of Advent that attention is focused on Christmas itself; then, in light of Christ's entrance in history, on how you will live throughout the new year. Such rehearsal and anticipation in constant flux seem to me to be what Advent is about.

I thank God for those who inspired me while writing the meditations. Some of the people will find themselves named and their stories told for our common growth in the faith. They are the saints of Central Presbyterian Church in Lafayette, Indiana, with whom I spent a glorious eighteen months as interim pastor.

Also, I could not have done the work without the help of Gladys Sargent. She pored over every page until it was right, shared with me her thoughts, made the necessary corrections, and otherwise nursed the project along until its completion. Our work together was that perfect combination of talents that comes with life in the Spirit and commitment to Christ's call. To her and to all I say, Thanks be to God.

Pentecost 16, 1988   J.G.K.

FIRST WEEK

Isaiah 2:1-5   First Week: Sunday

CULTIVATE

Isaiah's vision is of the time when the mountain of the Lord shall be established. The nations shall flow to it as people seek to learn of God's ways. The law of the Lord will judge all nations fairly. It will be a time when weapons are reforged into instruments for cultivating the land. In other words, the people will learn to cultivate mutual respect and understanding rather than dominate through destructive means.

Cultivate, don't dominate; that's the word for today! Isaiah's vision is a pastoral one; it is of a land cared for and treated in such a way that it can bear fruit. The vision is of those eager to learn God's will, to hear and obey God's word. The vision is of the Lord high and lifted up, surveying all lands and peoples equally, making fair judgments, according all the benefit of a wisdom that brings peace rather than bloodshed, reconciliation over against animosity: of the time when "the wolf shall dwell with the lamb, and the leopard shall lie down with the kid, and the calf and the lion and the fatling together, and a little child shall lead them" (Isa. 11:6). Cultivate the vision!

"Cultivate" has such positive connotations; it is a word that generates visions easily. It implies effort and a sense of not being satisfied with the status quo. It expresses direction, with the implication being that certain steps need to be taken in order to attain the desired result. It presupposes that the necessary implements are available—in Isaiah's case, plowshares and pruning hooks. It doesn't argue the fact that improvement is needed; without cultivation nothing that is sought may be attained.

"Dominate," on the other hand, has few redeeming qualities. To dominate is to stifle and impede growth, to rob whatever it may be of its natural abilities to generate unique results. It implies an overpowering presence that seeks to superimpose on another one's own intentions, values, or ways of doing things. Like cultivation, domination may get things done, but usually in a one-sided fashion.

Throughout the day, watch for those occasions to cultivate relationships and watch out for the times when to dominate is likely. Check on how the seeds of destruction are sown when domination seems to be prevalent. Lend a hand to those occasions when cultivation is occurring. In most cases the contrast will be evident; by their fruits we shall know them.

Cultivate, don't dominate friendships. Allow them to flourish as you tend to their growth. Cultivate reconciliation with those who may anger you; don't dominate them with spite or thoughts of revenge. Cultivate new insights that will enhance your perspective rather than dominate your opinions with attitudes unlikely to change. Cultivate mutual understanding between groups not attuned to each other, and don't let one or the other always dominate the scene.

Isaiah's vision was of a mountaintop experience where the people would go to learn new ways and walk along the Lord's pathways. To cultivate rather than dominate can have that kind of exhilaration to it, the rarefied air of walking in the midst of God's Spirit, experiencing new vistas, setting new sights, and seeing some things for the first time. Cultivate, don't dominate! It's the way of the Lord.

Herald of a new day and bringer of good tidings, we come bearing our gifts of thanksgiving and praise. Lift our sights to the high mountain, that we may learn of your ways and walk in your paths. Help us this day to follow in the footsteps of our Lord and Savior and be sustained by the indwelling of his Holy Spirit. For we pray in the name of Jesus, who taught his disciples to pray, saying: "Our Father who art in heaven, hallowed be thy name. Thy kingdom come, thy will be done, on earth as it is in heaven. Give us this day our daily bread; and forgive us our debts, as we forgive our debtors; and lead us not into temptation, but deliver us from evil. For thine is the kingdom and the power and the glory, forever. Amen."

SUPPLEMENT YOUR FAITH

Peter is zealous in listing those things that prevent Christians from being ineffective and unfruitful in the knowledge of our Lord Jesus Christ. He calls us to confirm our call and election, for in this way an entrance will be richly provided into the eternal kingdom of our Lord and Savior Jesus Christ. The list includes virtue, knowledge, self-control, steadfastness, godliness, brotherly affection, and love.

Supplement your faith with those attributes he lists, and the result will be an effective and fruitful witness to God's love and graciousness. Begin with virtue. Your virtue is what leads you to do well all that you do. It also leads to the well-being of others. With that in mind you could never speak about a terrorist's virtue. On the other hand, you could apply it to countless volunteers, who give of their time and talents in numerous humanitarian efforts.

Next comes knowledge. No one is ever too old to learn. Think of those in retirement homes and nursing homes whose minds are still alert. They refuse to relinquish their right to probe the mysteries of life. They pursue their quest with an enthusiasm born of the reality that time is running out.

Self-control hearkens back to the great commandment, especially the portion that reminds us to love our neighbors as ourselves. The more able we are to control that self, the more energy and ability we have for the neighbor. Maximum moderation in all things is still a piece of wise advice.

"Steadfastness" is one of those words we don't

ordinarily use. It reminds me of persons who are quite intentional and not prone to waver once their course is established. The opposite would be someone who was fickle and fainthearted. Peter would urge us to set our course and keep it true to our goal.

Godliness is nothing else than making it clear whose you are. All those attributes we assign to God have by grace been packaged in each one of us. Godliness is another way of saying, Do everything you do to God's honor and glory. After all, it was God who made us, and we are to place God in all that we do. What better way to do that than in a godly fashion?

Brotherly affection is a hallmark of our faith. It is one of the most common expressions for love in the New Testament. Brotherly affection is love at its broadest and comprehensive best, where we hold all people in esteem, bound together in common care and support.

Love is the *agape* of our faith in its deepest and most sacred sense, the love that is totally absorbing, unselfish, devoted, and true. As such, it is usually limited to those few we hold most dear in life, yet it was used by our Lord and his disciples as the epitome of love by which God sent Jesus into the world.

Add the attributes together and you achieve the composite of faith for which Peter was seeking: persons unswerving in loyalty to their neighbor and committed to increasing awareness of how they may serve Christ in everything they do, who act not out of any zeal for personal gain but in order to reflect the countless gifts God gives them through the grace of Christ. Now that's a fruitful and effective witness!

We greet the day, O God, with Christ's promise of new life before us. We pursue the day's course confident of your

Spirit's guidance. Not an hour goes by without our reliance upon your grace and mercy. You sustain us day in and day out, thanks to your love. Help us to augment our faith with those attributes that will make us more pleasing in your sight. Keep us from straying from your will for our lives. Make us more faithful, for in Christ's name we pray.

2 Peter 1:12-21   First Week: Tuesday

PAY ATTENTION

Peter wants everything to be well understood before he departs. Throughout today's scripture he admonishes his readers to pay attention to the things he has taught them. He reminds them that the truth of Christ is not just some myth; he himself was an eyewitness. He has heard the voice from heaven which proclaimed, "This is my beloved Son, with whom I am well pleased." Throughout his testimony, Peter never acts simply on his own impulse; he is led by the power of the Holy Spirit.

How well do you remember those times when you were admonished to "pay attention!" Flights of fancy were interrupted and you were brought back abruptly to the reality of the moment. Momentary dreams were left hanging in some form of suspended animation. Sometimes it was possible to recapture them; more often than not they were lost. You were reminded of more pressing concerns that required your attention, more pressing than those idyllic thoughts that so easily penetrated and captivated your consciousness.

Peter had a similar agenda. He had on his mind the need to clarify the nature of Jesus' appearance among them and its implications for their life as disciples. There would be those who claimed that his ministry was some sort of myth, a figment of Peter's imagination. Others might question Jesus' authority, as though it were fabricated in order to enhance the disciples' personal gain. Some might even assert that prophecy was simply impulsive and therefore judged incredible, to say the least. So Peter's agenda was for his readers to pay attention to the claims of the gospel before he departed.

Pay attention to the claims of the gospel. Claim one is Christ's power at work in your life. Hydroelectric plants are awesome marvels of engineering technology. They harness the energy of runaway streams and turn that energy into electrical power. Think of the creative power Christ has loosed in you through the gift of the Holy Spirit. As scripture reminds us, Jesus said, "Take my yoke upon you, and learn from me" (Matt. 11:29). Jesus harnesses each of us to himself, so that we may learn from him what faithfulness to God will mean day by day.

Claim two is the coming of our Lord Jesus Christ. As Paul writes in 1 Corinthians 13:12, "Now I know in part; then I shall understand fully, even as I have been fully understood." We yearn for the time when we shall fully understand the mysteries of God's love for us. In the meantime, we strive to live up to a measure of that love in the decisions we make, in our care for neighbors, in our dealings with strangers, and in our concern for the world.

Claim three is the prophetic word that continues to judge us as God's own and as such makes us accountable in thought, word, and deed. Peter referred to it as "a lamp shining in a dark place, until the day dawns and the morning star rises in your hearts." That prophetic word is capable of dispelling the shadows that continue to linger and cause doubt, misgivings, apprehension, and fear. That word can comfort us through nights of loneliness when sleep refuses to grant us escape from the cares and burdens that plague us. That word can bring us back to the stark reality that nothing in all of creation can ultimately separate us from God's love. That word is the same word that was borne to Jesus by the Majestic

Glory: "This is my beloved Son, with whom I am well pleased." We would do well to pay attention to that word.

"O Word of God incarnate, O Wisdom from on high, O Truth unchanged, unchanging, O Light of our dark sky, We praise you for the radiance that from the hallowed page, A lantern to our footsteps, shines on from age to age." Send forth that beacon of your holiness to guide our steps and show us the way. Enlighten our path and keep us from falling. Do not let us hide from your truth, but uphold us by your mercy as we seek to follow Christ in all that we do.

BEWARE

Peter cautions his readers to beware of scoffers. They will come in the last days and doubt the promise of Christ's coming. "Things haven't changed since the dawn of creation," they will say, "why should things be different now?" Peter reminds them that God's time is not our time, that God is merciful and seeks repentance, and that the last days will come as a thief in the night. In that sense all of us should beware of the unexpected.

"Beware" is one of those parental concerns that come from years of living. Our elders have passed through their times of trial and temptation. They have accrued years of experience and garnered a wisdom that they wear as though it were some garland strung about them. It is only natural that they seek to pass on to future generations the fruits of their labors.

Peter sought to do the same for his readers. He had been present at the trial of Jesus, was himself the victim of that odious temptation to deny his Lord. He had heard the taunts of the scoffers and perhaps joined in their chorus. But that was behind him now. He weathered the early times and was now living in the later times. If only he could impart to his readers some cautions that might keep them from falling away.

To beware in this sense is a parental or compassionate caution that someone bestows on another as a kind of protective security blanket. It may be said gently as a reminder to watch out for signs of impending danger. It may come in the form of a firm rebuke or admonition to cease and desist from pursuing perilous paths. In all cases, it should be received in the manner in which it is given, an intentional reminder from one who should know better not to engage in behavior that may imperil or damage another's future.

Scripture is full of such admonitions. They are not meant as restraints, as though faith is some sort of straitjacket meant to imprison free movement. Nor are they meant as scoldings delivered by some tyrannical overlord bent on whipping his charges into shape. They are the collective wisdom of those who have preceded us on an often turbulent journey, the summation of years spent seeking to be faithful, a compilation of the journey that shows what pitfalls to avoid and what paths not to take.

Peter was concerned with how things might occur in the last days and sought to prepare his readers so that they would not be misled. Remembering that God's time is not our time and that anxiety over such matters will not add one year to our life, it seems as though sound advice would be this: Live each day to the extent that if the end were to come you would not need to spend time apologizing for your misdeeds and feeling sorry about unmet opportunities. An old saying urges us to "seize the moment"; it is the moment that encapsulates all of life.

The warning to beware always needs to be set in the context of the wise admonition that reminds us not to "be anxious about your life, what you shall eat, nor about your body, what you shall put on. For life is more than food, and the body more than clothing. . . . Instead, seek God's kingdom, and these things shall be yours as well" (Luke 12:22-23, 31). "Beware" is an admonition to avoid whatever may threaten your life in God's kingdom.

Borne aloft by your mercy, O God, we are uplifted by your Spirit and held in the cradling embrace of your compassion and care. Continue to guide us by your wisdom, that our feet do not stumble along our journey of faith. Keep us from seeking vain signs that may misguide us, and help us look to Jesus who is the pioneer of our faith. We thank you for those beacons that have gone before us and that today light our path in our quest of the faith.

2 Peter 3:11-18   First Week: Thursday

GROW IN GRACE
AND KNOWLEDGE
OF JESUS CHRIST

Peter concludes his second letter with some last-minute instructions. We await new heavens and a new earth where righteousness dwells. In the meantime, we are to be zealous to be found by Christ without spot or blemish. Christ's forbearance is our salvation, since Christ himself endured even the cross on our behalf. We are to grow in the grace and knowledge of our Lord and Savior, to whom be the glory now and forever.

Harry Emerson Fosdick writes, "The difficulty in our expansive modern life lies here: ever achieving new powers, enlarging our opportunities, widening our liberties and everywhere complicating our lives, we forget that, unless we correspondingly strengthen our moral and spiritual foundations, the whole overextended superstructure will come down about our ears, as did the old Philistine banquet hall when Samson broke the pillars" (*Twelve Tests of Character,* Association Press, 1923; p. 21).

"Unless we correspondingly strengthen our moral and spiritual foundations." Increasingly we hear of persons suffering from burnout. Modern living causes stress. It is estimated that the average person endures three to four stressful situations weekly. The results are tension, frustration, and anger. Without some means to cope, those results begin to fester within us and eventually cause what Fosdick describes: "The whole overextended superstructure will come down about our ears."

Peter offers some words of guidance on how to

cope with stressful situations: "Grow in the grace and knowledge of our Lord and Savior Jesus Christ" (v. 18). To grow in grace is to remember that Christ sits at God's right hand and intercedes on our behalf. There is no limit to God's care for us, nor to Christ's compassion to aid us in dealing with our concerns. Keep communication open to God daily and lay before the throne of heaven those stress-causing situations. Whether by prayer, meditation, or silent reflection, soon you will notice the guidance that is forthcoming and the means available to ease the causes of your dis-ease.

Remember Ignatius of Loyola's dictum, "Pray as though everything depended on you and work as though everything depended on God." It is so easy to reverse the process and work ourselves into a frenzy, seeking to do everything by ourselves. Pray as though everything depended on you. Sort out what can be done now and what must await resolution. Resolve those current needs day by day, and God will grant strength sufficient to attain your goal. For then you will be working as though everything depended on God.

Peter admonishes his reader to "count the forbearance of our Lord as salvation" (v. 15). That should be good news. No longer do we need to save ourselves, since Christ has already achieved that goal on our behalf. No longer do we have to try to justify our existence in order to convince some heavenly bookkeeper that our ledger has more credits than debits. Our sins are forgiven and our shortcomings washed away by Christ's sacrifice on our behalf.

Socrates said, "Know thyself." Know the limits of your abilities, your boundaries of energy, and the capacity of your endeavors. Grow in the knowledge of Jesus Christ, and know yourself through his will for you. For then you will shore up those moral and spiritual foundations that will withstand the stresses of modern-day living.

Gracious God, who turns the shadows of doubt into daybreak and cleanses us of sin, we give you thanks for mercy and grace. Sustain us through times of peril and uphold us when we waver. Lift from us those burdens too heavy for us to shoulder and show us how to cope with our stress. Prepare us to do what you want us to do and go where you want us to go, that daily we may strive to be faithful to Christ, who calls to us, "Come, follow me."

PRACTICE PATIENCE

The psalmist speaks today to those who fret. The message is basically this: Do not fret over those who seem to get ahead because of wicked or underhanded ways. It is better to trust in the Lord and commit your way to God. God will give you the desires of your heart, maybe not today or tomorrow, but in God's time and according to the way of the Lord. The admonition is to wait patiently upon the Lord and "fret not yourself; it tends only to evil" (v. 8).

Patience is heralded throughout the pages of scripture. The seed planted in good soil bears fruit with patience (Luke 8:15). Ecclesiastes reminds us that "the patient in spirit is better than the proud in spirit" (Eccl. 7:8). Isaiah's famous counsel is that "they who wait for the LORD shall renew their strength, they shall mount up with wings like eagles, they shall run and not be weary, they shall walk and not faint" (Isa. 40:31). Paul was convinced that "suffering produces endurance, and endurance produces character, and character produces hope, and hope does not disappoint us, because God's love has been poured into our hearts through the Holy Spirit which has been given to us" (Rom. 5:3-5). Throughout scripture there is the sense that we are not to be anxious. Be about your tasks daily and you will reap the benefits of your labor.

Patience is the active pursuit of a goal you wish to attain. In that sense, patience takes practice. Instant gratification is like the lottery; the odds against your achieving it are high. When I was a child I wanted everything now; there was no time to wait, and why couldn't I have what I wanted? As years passed I learned that I could; it would only take time, effort, and work day by day to achieve it.

Currently a friend of mine is building a log house, the type that comes delivered with all the logs numbered and notched to fit snugly together. She told me that it took four days to sort and stack the logs on the house's foundation near where they would fit. Then day by day the process continued of placing each log in its proper position on top of the last. Soon a room took shape, then another and another. The time came for the roof's support beams to be positioned and then the roof could be added, the windows inserted, and the doors hung. When everything was assembled it was remarkable how each piece fit together to produce a well-built house. Now my friend and her family can finish and furnish the interior.

Her description reminded me of playing with Lincoln Logs. As a youth how I loved to construct cabins, houses, and fortresses in much the same fashion. Today, it is Legos that hold our children's attention. Maybe I was learning to practice patience all along!

Life offers a similar sense of construction, as we build log upon log until the goal is achieved. To yearn for the result without labor is fruitless and will yield only frustration. To cut short the process and bypass a necessary step might hasten completion but in the end weaken the total effect.

The psalmist says to trust in the Lord, take delight in the Lord, commit your way to the Lord, and be still before the Lord. That's a good prescription for practicing patience. For God will provide strength, endurance, character, and hope. Those, combined with our efforts, assure us that the work will get done. Don't fret!

Benevolent Architect of the universe, who formed the seas and dry land, who brooded over the beasts of the field and birds of the air, who fashioned us after your image and breathed into your creation the breath of life, we worship and bow down before you. Give us strength to pursue the tasks before us, the humility to recognize our limitations, the wisdom to correct our errors, and the patience to persevere. May all we say and do be in accordance with your creative goodness and bring you all glory and honor.

SEEK JUSTICE
AND RIGHTEOUSNESS

Amos deals a devastating blow to those who would allow their worship of God to be confined to some stereotypical forms of adoration and praise. He takes no delight in feasts or solemn assemblies. He wants nothing to do with offerings given as though to appease God's wrath. He would also just as soon do without the noisy songs and clanging cymbals. What for him is adequate homage to the sovereign Lord is the constant search for justice and a pervasive quest after righteousness.

In that sense worship is meant to be the order of the day each day of the week. According to the psalmist, righteousness and justice are the foundation of God's throne, with steadfast love and faithfulness its constant companion (Ps. 89:14). The psalmist enjoins us to "give justice to the weak and the fatherless; maintain the right of the afflicted and the destitute. Rescue the weak and the needy; deliver them from the hand of the wicked" (Ps. 82:3-4). The poet advises a just balance in all our affairs and warns against false pride, the shallow security of riches, the needless belittling of one's neighbor, and the spread of malicious gossip (Prov. 11:1-19). Jesus, of course, summarized the cause of justice and righteousness in the Sermon on the Mount: Do unto others as you would have them do unto you (Matt. 7:12).

To seek justice and righteousness is somewhat akin to waking to the dawn of a new day. You hope the night has brought refreshment and rest. You have been born again from sleep and been granted a new day by God's grace. Throughout its course there will be constant reminders of God's mercy showered upon you, as you bathe, dress, eat, and go about your assigned tasks. To seek justice and righteousness is to grant unto others those same abilities and blessings and to work toward their bestowal upon those who despair of receiving them.

Paul had a lot to say about righteousness. Christ came to set us aright. Thereafter we live by grace and have no boast in ourselves alone, but only through Christ who lives in us. So all that we are and do should reflect that mercy which God has bestowed upon us. Of what value is it then to deny others those same gifts we have received? Shouldn't we, rather, reflect that same love in our normal dealings with neighbors that God has seen fit to reflect in Christ, the Light of the world? "Do not yield your members to sin as instruments of wickedness, but yield yourselves to God . . . as instruments of righteousness" (Rom. 6:13). For Paul, to dwell in Christ was to seek justice and righteousness.

Life is like an ever-flowing stream. There are eddies and shoals, there are the refreshing times of deep waters along with the turbulence of the rapids. Sometimes the pace is breathtaking as the waters race over the rocks; other times there is the serenity of a liquid pool shaded from the blazing heat of the noonday sun. The stream is never still but is constantly changing, eventually to sacrifice itself within the course of a mighty river or the depths of the great ocean. But always each drop will retain its unique identity, born as the rain or some tiny gurgling spring pushed up from the earth's hidden depths, only to be joined with all the other drops in the course of its journey.

Amos saw the pursuit of justice and righteousness

as being as normal as the course of life itself. That is what worship should be: giving to God what God has already bestowed upon us. As we approach the throne of grace, let us hold up before us that same quest after justice and righteousness that is as normal as the flow of life.

O God, with what shall we come into your presence and bow down before you? You have shown us what is good: to do justice, to love kindness, and to walk humbly with you. Let us not be satisfied with solemn assemblies but let our festal shouts be in pursuit of your justice and peace. Help us to set aright what is askew, and keep us upright and gracious in all our dealings. Let us truly seek to do unto others as we would have them do unto us.

SECOND WEEK

Romans 15:4-13   Second Week: Sunday

ABOUND IN HOPE

The vision is of God who abounds with steadfastness and encouragement. The people are encouraged
to live in harmony with their neighbors. There is
every reason to welcome one another, since Christ
has welcomed you. The purpose is to glorify God,
the source of hope who can fill you with all joy and
peace in believing, so that by the power of the Holy
Spirit you may abound with the same steadfastness
and encouragement.

Jody is the vivacious mother of three grown
daughters, all raised and out of the nest. She was
looking forward to growing old together with her
husband, aware of the importance of each day they
spent together. Five years ago, time's importance became real to her when she underwent surgery to
have a breast removed due to cancer. A few weeks
ago she had another lump removed that was likewise
diagnosed as malignant.

A group of us sat with her husband during the
outpatient surgery. We were there when the surgeon
came and told Dave that initial tests showed this
latest lump to be a continuation of her disease. We
were there when Jody herself joined us, a little wob-
bly from her ordeal but nevertheless realistic about
her future. It would take a week before the final
results were known. In the meantime, the next day
she would begin a series of further tests to determine
the extent of the disease and what possible courses
of treatment would be prescribed. She never lost
hope and, in fact, was a source of steadfastness and

encouragement to the small group of supporters surrounding her husband.

The next day there were phone calls to make. The parish was informed, and friends promised to surround her with their company and assistance. The daughters were alerted, but not alarmed unduly. Their grandmother was called. She thought it would be nice to send Jody and Dave on a cruise, just to let them get away and spend time with each other. Jody went for her tests and found that the disease could initially be treated with hormones. There was no guarantee that she would be cured, but at least there was hope: hope for remission and hope for some years in which she and Dave could grow old together.

How fragile life is! Sometimes it takes this fragility for hope to abound, for people to rely on God's steadfastness and encouragement, to comprehend how important it is to dwell in harmony with one another. Paul wrote in order to break down the wall of hostility between Jews and Gentiles. Christ came as a servant to the circumcised and a source of mercy to the Gentiles. Henceforth, all peoples, whether Jew or Gentile, slave or free, male or female, well or sick, would know the testimony of the scriptures: God was in Christ, reconciling the world to God's glory and honor.

To abound in hope when all about us seems to be crumbling is the real testimony to Christ's presence among us. Jody remains steadfast in her conviction that she will be healed. Dave continues to receive encouragement from the men and women of the parish. They have both altered their life-styles to spend more time with each other and to visit their family. They take each day as it comes, empowered by the Spirit to endure its trials.

To abound in hope is to approach walls of hostility

infused with the power of Christ's reconciling love and to surmount them with all joy and peace in believing. We continue to marvel at Jody's spirit throughout her trials. But then, why should we marvel? God's gift is for us too.

Patterned after your goodness, O God, we seek to live by your grace. Your mercy surrounds us; it enfolds us like a blanket while we are sleeping and protects us like armor when awake. May we never take for granted your benevolent care of us, but morning and evening give you all praise and thanksgiving. Help us throughout the course of this day to remain steadfast in our faith and a source of encouragement to others, to work for peace among our neighbors, and to radiate the joy of believing in your Son, Jesus Christ.

Luke 1:57-68   Second Week: Monday

CLAIM YOUR INHERITANCE

Questions arise over what to call Elizabeth's child. Some suggest Zechariah, after his father. Elizabeth chooses the name John, and her husband agrees. As soon as Zechariah has written the name on a tablet he regains his voice and speaks, praising God: "Blessed be the Lord God of Israel, for he has visited and redeemed his people." God's benediction is bestowed on the people, a blessing that will in time be fulfilled in the life, death, and resurrection of Jesus Christ.

Carol first came to the church office seeking assistance. She and her husband were about to be evicted from their apartment. They needed housing, work, and some means to meet the mounting bills. Carol was street-wise and knew how to use the social agency system. She was also scared. So many times she had received promises, but strings were attached. She had in her brief twenty-two years of life suffered sufficient abuse to be wary, but she also knew she needed help.

The offer was made that if she were to work at the church part-time as a housekeeper, the church would find her the assistance she required. The staff took her under their wing and began to train her and give her responsibility. Periodically, she rebelled and refused to follow procedures. Her supervisors were relentless and just as stubborn in their care about her and for her. At one point she left, convinced that she could do better elsewhere, only to return and admit that no one had ever cared for her as much as the church. That day she realized God's blessing; she was a part of Christ's family.

Tragically, four months later both her father and stepmother were killed in a head-on collision. The church was there to console and comfort her, embrace her with their love for her, and see to it that her immediate needs were met. What she had realized from a biblical point of view now became a physical reality: The church was her closest remaining family.

Carol went on to learn how to operate the offset printer and has become proficient in a marketable skill. Soon she may leave the church for more lucrative positions of employment, but she will never leave the embrace of the congregation's care and concern for her. She will retain her family ties as a child of God who experienced personally God's love in Christ's body, the church.

Elizabeth and Zechariah experienced that same love in the birth of the son they chose to call John. Zechariah heralded the day as a sign of God's benediction over the people. John would go before to prepare the Lord's ways, to give knowledge of salvation to the people, the forgiveness of sins, and to guide their feet to the Prince of Peace.

The church inherits that promise through Christ and has as one of its responsibilities to proclaim to the people, "Come, claim your inheritance." Carol's knowledge of salvation began when someone cared enough to seek shelter and food for her and her husband. She began to believe that her sins were forgiven as she shared some of her past as well as present and in so doing found acceptance and support. She learned to accept the peace that came with responsibly fulfilling those tasks assigned to her and took pride in her growth as others recognized her achievements. Carol is reborn into a life full of grace and mercy and can truly say, "Blessed be the Lord God of Israel, for he has visited and redeemed his people."

O God, you claim and name us and make us your own. You do not withhold your love from us but, as a parent, gather us under the protective shield of your love. Where can we go that you do not find us; what can we do that you do not chasten and guide us? Help us to live worthy of your benediction and faithful to Christ's call to love and obey. As we claim our inheritance as your sons and daughters, let us pass on to others that same acceptance and care.

Matthew 22:34-46   Second Week: Tuesday

LOVE YOUR NEIGHBOR
AS YOURSELF

Jesus is confronted by the Pharisees and the Sad-
ducees. They have a question for him: "Which is the
great commandment in the law?" Jesus rehearses for
them how they should love God with all their heart,
soul, and mind. They should also love their neighbors as themselves. It's as simple as that! The entire
law and the prophets depend on such a simple equation. However, as is so often the case, what is so
easily said is hard to accomplish.

As an example, for a moment put yourself in the
center of your universe. Many people find it difficult
to love themselves. For some reason they yearn to be
like others; they are dissatisfied with their looks,
their status in life, their attributes, their abilities.
They wish things were different. Or throughout
much of the day they dwell on "if only." If only such
and such would happen; if only something else were
not the case; if only they could achieve whatever.
Whatever the cause, they bemoan their plight and
yearn for the day when things will be different.

In that case, such people would find it difficult to
love their neighbor. They can't muster the courage to
love themselves. They are typically found belittling
others, since they have such a low opinion of themselves. To elevate others would only compound their
own lack of esteem, in which they find themselves
mired and unable to escape.

To such as these Jesus' admonition would be, Look
to God with all your heart, soul, and mind. See what
God has done on your behalf, the limits to which

God has gone to rescue you from the pit of self-pity and degradation, the heights to which God elevates you through Christ's resurrection, the assurance of God's eternal presence promised through the gift of the Holy Spirit. Then be lifted up and strengthened to show a measure of that same esteem showered upon you as you reach out to your neighbor with acceptance and care.

Others cannot get beyond the love they lavish on themselves. Their egos demand constant gratification, their desires are unquenchable, and they always make their wills known. They are not prone to lavish others with favors but grasp as much as they can for themselves. Their field of vision is often limited to the myopia of their own desires, and the periphery of another's concerns is often shut out of sight.

Jesus would accuse those persons of idolatry and criticize them harshly for their unwarranted egoism. After all, is it not God who is the giver of every good and perfect gift? Has not God made them a little less than the angels and appointed them stewards over all creation? And will not God remain the sole judge of those Jesus taught to visit the sick, protect the homeless, comfort the bereaved, and care for the oppressed? Even if it were but a portion of what they reserved for themselves, think of the love they could heap on their neighbors!

Many of us fit in neither the one nor the other extreme category. Our days are spent seeking to do our tasks decently, giving God glory, and building for ourselves some sense of security. We do what we can to help others, and sometimes the scope of the task seems overwhelming. There aren't enough hours in the day, nor do we have the strength or ability to do what needs to be done. In that case Luther's famous saying applies: Love God with all your heart, soul, and mind—and then do as you please! Inevitably God's will will be done and our neighbor's needs will be met. To God be the honor and praise!

Merciful God, your bountiful care is as far-reaching as the heavens and your love extends to the depths of the sea; you shower us with your blessings and look after our needs. You sent Jesus that we may have life, and that abundantly. You surround us with the Holy Spirit, that we may be led by your will. Make us mindful of the needs of our neighbors and let us look after their cares, that we may reflect your benevolence and obey your commands. Help us to comfort the lonely, feed the hungry, and accept the stranger, for as we do so unto even the least of these we shall do so unto Christ, in whose name we pray.

Matthew 23:1-12   Second Week: Wednesday

BE HUMBLE

Jesus teaches the crowds and his disciples to be humble. The theme is that the greatest among them shall be their servant. Others will do deeds in order to be commended; they will glory in being seated at the place of honor; they will boast of their accomplishments and be known by their titles. But such fame shall not benefit them before God's throne of judgment. Rather, "whoever exalts himself will be humbled, and whoever humbles himself will be exalted."

There is a vast difference between humility and humiliation. Jesus sought humility from his disciples since he took humiliation upon himself. He was willing to undergo the taunts of the crowds and the jeers of the bystanders, so that those who believed in him could boast of the Lord and not take pride in themselves. Thereafter no one ever again need taste the bitterness of humiliation alone; it was accomplished once and for all. Those who would follow him were taught to be humble, since they themselves had done nothing to gain their salvation.

As the saying goes, "What's bred in the bone will not out of the flesh." Humility is part of our breeding as Christians. Paul recounts how Jesus "humbled himself and became obedient unto death, even death on a cross" (Phil. 2:8). James reminds us that "God opposes the proud, but gives grace to the humble" (James 4:6). "Humble yourselves before the Lord and he will exalt you" (James 4:10). Paul finds the roots of humility in God's call itself: "Not many of you were wise according to worldly standards; not many were powerful, not many were of noble birth; but God chose what is foolish in the world to shame the wise, God chose what is weak in the world to shame the strong" (1 Cor. 1:26-27). So if there is to be any boasting, let whoever boasts, boast of the Lord. Such teaching is inbred in Christians from an early age.

Pride is insidious, though, and the slightest accomplishment tempts us to forget what we've learned. Soon we begin to believe that abilities are rightfully ours and no amount of mercy and grace has gotten us where we are. We forget the care it has taken to perfect those skills, often at the expense of some teacher's patience. We even begin to accept the fact that, once learned, such abilities will always sustain their perfection without further training or practice. That is when we usually experience what is called the "humility factor." Something occurs to bring us down off our sense of self-esteem and elation, and we are humbled at the expense of that false sense of self-pride. Jesus sought to avoid for his disciples those experiences of the humility factor and would have them be humble in graciously accepting their gifts.

Dag Hammarskjöld, in his book *Markings,* asks the question, "Do you still need to evoke memories of self-imposed humiliation in order to extinguish a smoldering self-admiration?" He then goes on to give some advice: "To be pure in heart means, among other things, to have freed yourself from all such half-measures: from a tone of voice which places you in the limelight, a furtive acceptance of some desire of the flesh which ignores the desire of the spirit, a self-righteous reaction to others in their moments of weakness. Look at yourself in *that* mirror when you wish to be praised—or to judge" (Alfred A. Knopf, 1964; p. 109).

What's bred in the bone may come out in the flesh!
Be humble, and God will exalt you to the end that
God's name be praised.

*Where would we be without your divine favor, O God?
Indeed, who could live apart from your grace? Yet you have
seen fit to shower us with blessings and impart to us all we
could ever want or need. Help us to live simply in reliance
upon your goodness and to chart our course faithfully according to your will. Keep us from vain boasting of our own
sense of grandeur, from false pride that elevates us at the
expense of our neighbor, from self-esteem without thought
of Christ's sacrifice for us, and from any hindrance to giving
you all glory and honor.*

Jeremiah 31:16-22   Second Week: Thursday

FOLLOW THE GUIDEPOSTS

Jeremiah foresees the time when Israel will return from exile. He writes of Ephraim's repentance: how Ephraim was chastened, ashamed, and confounded. God remembers the Israelites and will have mercy on them. In the meantime they are to make for themselves guideposts, waymarks so they do not repeat their errant ways. "Consider well the highway, the road by which you went." It is another way of saying, "Learn from your mistakes."

Guideposts abound. Some tell us what we should do, others tell us what we better not do. Some tell us directions and how far we still have to travel. Others make suggestions, advice we ought to follow. By and large, every guidepost is the result of someone's experience, a testimony to the fact that others who have traveled before us want to pass on some wisdom to those who follow.

One guidepost, for example, is YIELD. At times it's best to give way to others who have the right of way. Now, that by no means implies we have no right to be on the road. It's just a gentle reminder to wait until traffic clears before getting into the thick of things. Life is a process of learning how to yield to those with experience. Soon your time will come to be in the mainstream, and others will yield to your direction. However, sometimes we're tempted to plunge headlong without surveying the traffic, only to find that our haste causes disruption and some degree of confusion. To yield takes patience and wisdom. With practice you learn how to gauge the traffic and when to make your move.

Another well-known guidepost is DETOUR AHEAD. How often has that occurred, much to your consternation! What could have been a straight line from here to there becomes a series of right-angle turns that seemingly cause undue delay. However, consider the danger if the sign is not heeded. It's there for a reason, and to ignore it would be foolish. Life, as well, is a series of detours. They are meant in most cases to protect us from potential hazards. Sometimes their cause is beyond our control. Like the YIELD guidepost, DETOUR does not imply we won't get where we're going. It may take us a bit out of the way, but in the end we'll arrive safely and be better for having obeyed the sign.

A third guidepost is DEAD END. There's no sense pursuing the course because it doesn't go anywhere. There's no way out except retracing your steps. Linked to DEAD END is U-TURN, the classic guidepost for repentance. To repent often implies a complete about-face. How many times has life offered dead ends without any chance for an exit? To pursue such paths will be perilous at best and disastrous at worst. The only possible course of action is to make that about-face and head in a different direction.

CURVE has a way of causing us to proceed with caution. Unfortunately, life is never a straight line from one point to another. The terrain is such that there are hills as well as valleys and numerous obstacles to get around. The curves in life provide an opportunity to slow your pace and enjoy the scenery.

Fortunately, the speed zones remind us not to let the pace of living get out of hand. As Ecclesiastes reminds us, "For everything there is a season, and a time for every matter under heaven" (Eccl. 3:1). The guideposts are there for a reason, and throughout life we learn to be guided by the directions they appropriately convey.

Gracious God, we thank you for your guiding hand through life. You know when to chasten and when to confound us; you know how to uplift us and set our spirits soaring. You have given us the law and the prophets and sent Christ to live among us. You have made your way known and bade us follow. Help us along the way to heed your direction, to be led by the wisdom of your Holy Spirit, and to repent of our errors when we disobey your will. Guide us to the gates of your kingdom, that we may dwell in your favor and inherit your promise of life without end.

KNOW THE LORD

"Behold, the days are coming, says the LORD, when I will make a new covenant with the house of Israel and the house of Judah." Jeremiah then conveys just what the new covenant implies: God will put the law within them and will write it upon their hearts. They will be God's people and will know the Lord, from the least of them to the greatest. God will forgive their iniquity and will no longer remember their sin. Truly, Jeremiah's vision is of a new day.

Know the Lord. What an ominous task! Yet, as Jeremiah reminds us, no longer will anyone teach their neighbor to know the Lord, since all will know God. Obviously we have not yet arrived at such comprehensive knowledge. The task is yet before us.

That's not to say that events have not occurred in history to make the task easier. God sent the Son, who came and walked among us. The Bible is a living legacy to the Word made flesh and contains the authoritative witness to Christ's teachings and the testimonies of his disciples and followers.

To know the Lord is faithfully to read the accounts of the early church. There is still no substitute for disciplined daily reading of scripture. Just as you are doing today, let the words leap off the page and embrace you with God's timeless truths. Let them speak to you of the biblical writer's own faith and commitment. Let them inspire you to God's own faithfulness down through the ages. Let them guide you to your own zealous obedience. Let them confront as well as comfort you as you pursue your own journey of discipleship.

To know the Lord is to be led by the guidance of the Holy Spirit. As Jesus neared the end of his time on earth, he taught that the Counselor would come. During each year, we celebrate Pentecost on the fiftieth day of Easter, when the people spoke, each in their own tongue. They were inflamed with new zeal to proclaim the good news of the gospel. Since then the Spirit has been there to goad us, cajole us, guide us, and surround us. The Spirit enlivens us today as it did back then, as we, the church, seek to be faithful to Christ's call.

To know the Lord is to be guided by the confessions of the church, ecumenical documents written by Christ's faithful followers seeking to address particular issues and meet specific needs. Based on scripture, these confessions have been handed down from generation to generation and today provide a collective witness to those who have preceded us on their own quest to be faithful. Confessions can be useful guides in our daily encounter with God's will for our lives.

To know the Lord is to "rejoice always, pray constantly, give thanks in all circumstances; for this is the will of God in Christ Jesus for you" (1 Thess. 5:16-18). How often is the troubled heart brought to rest through some moments spent in prayer. Fervent desires are confidently placed at the feet of the omnipotent God, with the assurance that Christ sits at God's right hand and intercedes on our behalf. There is no care too heavy or joy so sublime that it cannot be shared with God, who yearns to hear from us.

To know the Lord may indeed sound awesome, yet each time we hear the cry of a newborn child we know God is near. Whenever we reach out to comfort the afflicted we obey God's commands. "Behold, the days are coming"—they may not yet be upon us, but they have begun—when God will write a new law on our hearts: Emmanuel, God with us.

O God, we have been taught to rejoice always, pray constantly, and give thanks in all circumstances. We rejoice always at the blessings you mercifully bestow on us. We pray constantly that your will be done on earth as it is in heaven. We give thanks in all circumstances, knowing that in all things you work together for good with those who love you. Write the new covenant on our hearts that we may come to know you in thought, word, and deed and give you the praise and honor due your glorious name.

Matthew 13:44-51   Second Week: Saturday
SEEK THE PEARL

Couched amid the parables of the kingdom is that
of the pearl. The merchant in search of a fine pearl
will sell all she or he has in order to purchase it.
Similarly, when people find treasure in a field they
will sell all they have in order to buy the field. Fish-
ermen will sort out their catch at the end of the day;
they will keep what is good and throw away the bad.
The kingdom of heaven is worth seeking, getting,
and keeping.

An article by a fellow minister reminded me a
while ago about the value of pearls. The Gemological
Institute of America describes the pearl as a symbol
of modesty and purity, "suggesting every color of
the rainbow, but always faintly, as if under pale
moonlight." As such, the pearl makes a classic state-
ment likewise about the kingdom of heaven. There
is nothing stark about the way the kingdom encompasses nature. It encompasses the creation with sub-
tlety and yet a certain richness.

The pearl seeks to persuade the viewer rather than
overwhelm. Unlike more dazzling jewelry, it tends to
blend in with what is being worn rather than stand
out and call attention to itself. As Matthew writes
elsewhere, "Seek first his kingdom and his righteousness, and all these things shall be yours as well"
(Matt. 6:33). Or, "When you pray, you must not be
like the hypocrites; for they love to stand and pray
in the synagogues and at the street corners, that they
may be seen by men. Truly, I say to you, they have
received their reward" (Matt. 6:5). The kingdom of

heaven and God's righteousness should be worn like
fine pearls and not call attention to themselves.

The pearl is the softest of all gems. On Mohs' scale
of hardness, which runs from 1 to 10, talc is softest,
diamond is hardest, and pearl is about 3. Pearls can
be easily scratched and shattered. Care needs to be
taken when wearing them, or their luster will be
impaired. However, the more they are worn the
greater becomes their translucent beauty. As with
God's kingdom, neglect can do them more harm than
good and cause their luster to fade.

Remember also that pearls are the product of irritation within the mollusk. So often, we in the church
seek to avoid conflict. Irritating situations disturb us
and we seek a life free from disorder and hassle.
However, we would do well, like the oyster, to take
those gritty occasions and enfold ourselves around
them in order to produce gems of beauty rather than
just mere grains of sand.

The warm radiance of pearls inspires intimacy
over and above the cold brilliance of diamonds and
emeralds. Pearls are the result of an interchange between a living creature and its environment. So also
the kingdom is the result of the interplay between
God and creation. No amount of irritation could dis-
suade God from working for good with all that God
created. The patience it takes to produce fine pearls
is minor in comparison to the patience God has exer-
cised with us. The fruits of the kingdom can indeed
be likened to a string of matched pearls. Their creation is the result of interdependence and care.

So the next time you see the pearl, think of God's
kingdom. Seek pearls in life, be they in modesty and
purity, during moments of gentle persuasion, or re-
taining the luster of when you first believed. Embrace all of life in such a way that even the grit can

become a gem that suggests every color of the rainbow.

Gracious God, we come rough-hewn to the workbench of your mercy, there to be shaped and worked according to your infinite design. Take us and mold us as in Christ you have called us; make us in the image of what you would have us become. Remove those splinters in us that harm others, and soften the rough edges that cause them pain. Help us to be faithful to your design of the covenant and thereby inherit the kingdom Christ lived to proclaim.

THIRD WEEK

Isaiah 35:1-10   Third Week: Sunday

PREPARE
FOR GOD'S REIGN

Isaiah treats the reader to a glorious vision of what's in store for the people of God. Weak hands are strengthened, feeble knees are made firm. The blind see and the deaf hear. What was once dry land abounds with lush foliage, and the burning sands become a cool oasis. To get there, pilgrims travel over a way that is called holy. They will not encounter ravenous beasts on their journey but will reach their goal with joy and gladness. All sorrow and sighing shall flee away.

Life is a glorious venture for the wandering people of God. They begin their travels with the waters of baptism as a symbol of their past, having been cleansed through Christ's gracious act of forgiveness. Think of the countless women and men who have undergone such an initiation down through the ages! They have faithfully journeyed, often not without trial and never without pain. They have faithfully stayed the course and have themselves become a living testimony to the merciful God whose Spirit accompanied them.

As a child Pauline suffered the crippling effects of polio. She was thereafter confined to a wheelchair. Yet her hands remained strong and her voice never wavered. She became a music teacher and throughout her life taught countless pupils to play and sing. She would ask her pupils for a commitment to practice a required number of hours each day. What she expected was the same endurance she herself epitomized, and she gained the respect of all those under her tutelage. Her life was a testimony to a faith that gave strength to those she knew.

Art and Leora were told early in their marriage that they could never have their own children. As it turns out they have legions scattered throughout the United States. Art loved to collect stamps and seized an opportunity to train young minds to the adventures to be gained through the pursuit of philately. As Leora wooed the junior high youths to their house with delectables from her kitchen, Art trained their minds on the finer points of philatelic wisdom. Soon the house proved too small, and the crowd gathered in the church basement. Today, Art and Leora spend their retirement keeping track of their family and sharing the pains and the joys of the children they helped to raise.

At ninety years of age, Ruth's eyesight was not what it used to be. Yet she still served as an elder on the session of her church. She was not afraid to tackle the details of church leadership and took delight in keeping up to date on significant issues. When asked to participate in the Tenebrae service during Holy Week, she volunteered to read the last lesson, when the church would be dark. She memorized the scripture and for a week practiced her steps to the lectern. When she finally read the lesson there was not a sound save her firm voice. Till her death, Ruth remained a living testimony to the faith that can make us strong.

To prepare for God's reign is to live life to its fullest. In everyone's life there are mentors who have paved the way for our own journey. They have taken the time to strengthen weak knees and make firm our hands. They have opened our eyes to the wide vistas of God's encompassing creation. They have taught us to hear truths we might have otherwise ignored.

They have showed us how to reach the lush pastures and avoid the barren wastelands.

All this they have done out of commitment to the Christ who also spent time on the journey. Because of their time with us we are enabled to go and do likewise. Thereby we too will prepare for God's reign with those who will follow.

God of the prophets and poets, God of the wise and the faithful, God of all creation and judge over all, we thank you for the testimony of those whose journey is now over. For them death is past and their pain ended. They now rest eternally with you, thanks to Christ's promise of eternal life. May the lessons they taught us become the fabric of our daily lives, so entwined in us that the threads we weave reflect their wisdom and care. Make of our collective journeys a tapestry of faith dedicated to giving you all glory and honor.

Hebrews 4:1-13   Third Week: Monday

ENTER GOD'S REST

The author of Hebrews admonishes the reader not to fail to enter God's rest. It has to do with hearing the good news and believing what you hear. There are those in the past who heard it and did not believe it. Don't let that happen to you! The good news is this: God rested from work when the creation was complete. God did all that was necessary and then sent Jesus Christ into the world, that all who believe in him may have life and that, indeed, abundantly.

Just relax! Don't get uptight! Go with the flow! Do not be anxious about your life! Live life to the fullest! Today is the first day of the rest of your life! These modern-day admonitions are similar to what the author of Hebrews wrote long ago. They all say the same thing: To be anxious about your life will not add one speck of meaning or longevity. It may just do the opposite.

"Strive to enter God's rest" is a strange message to hear on Monday. Many of us have just spent the weekend relaxing, and now it is time to turn our sights to the workweek ahead. Relaxation is over and it's off to work we go. Yet the message is not meant to be that strange. If God rested when the creation was completed, what can we possibly do to improve on God's work? Shouldn't Monday through Friday rather be spent in caring for the gifts God has given us? In that sense, our workweek would be nothing more than a continuation of our Sunday worship, thanksgiving to God and praising God's name in all that we do.

Ah, but we know that things are not yet as they should be. There is still hunger and suffering. There are those on the streets unable to break out of the cycle of poverty; they need care and attention. AIDS and drugs continue to haunt us as the plagues did our foremothers and forefathers. There is still no peace in the land even though we are wiser to the threats of annihilation from war. What from God's side was completed and good, from humankind's point of view is not yet as it should be. So there is still work to be done, not to improve on what God did but to get it to where God intended the creation to be.

That is where Jesus Christ comes in. Those who read the scriptures hear that Christ is the way, the truth, and the life. Christ's way is sacrificial. He used the servant, steward, and shepherd as examples of the way we should behave toward our neighbors. They all imply that we should take care to put the well-being of others at least on the same level as our own, if not, indeed, ahead of our own. Christ's truth is that, in fact, we cannot save ourselves from God's judgment. Only God can do that and has already done so for those who believe in Christ as their Lord and Savior. So no amount of good works or riches will add one hour to our life span.

Life is to be lived with assurance that our sins are forgiven. Freed from their burden, we are then yoked with Christ in service on behalf of our neighbors and all of creation. We are to tend to one another's cares and concerns as we toil amid the wonders of science, technology, and modern-day problems. We know that Christ intercedes with God on our behalf through the Holy Spirit, who guides, energizes, and directs our efforts. And so we can rest assured at the end of the day that our efforts were to God's honor and glory. Strive to enter that rest!

God of all glory, your graciousness surrounds us, your love redeems us. Where would we be without your care? You have seen fit to send Christ into the world, that we may dwell in the light of your glorious redemption. Keep us from taking undue satisfaction in our own endeavors, and help us to work where we can be of use to others. Make of us better stewards of the benevolence you grant us and better servants of others when we see them in need. Let us rest assured of your mercy toward us and thereby love our neighbors as Christ taught us to do.

Hebrews 5:11–6:12   Third Week: Tuesday

WATCH WHAT YOU EAT

There's been some problem with those to whom Hebrews was written. The author accuses them of having become dull of hearing. By this time they should be teachers, chewing the solid food of the gospel; instead, they still need to drink the milk of God's goodness. There is no time for sluggishness when it comes to witnessing to Christ's righteousness. Lay aside dead works and cling to the full assurance of hope. For therein lies our ability to grow in the faith.

The author of Hebrews would probably agree wholeheartedly with today's adage, "You are what you eat"! The problem with many in the community to whom the letter was sent was they were not eating enough solid food. When it came to matters of Christ's teachings, they were content to stay on the bland diet "of repentance from dead works and of faith toward God, with instruction about ablutions, the laying on of hands, the resurrection of the dead, and eternal judgment" (6:1-2). While all this might be necessary, and definitely true, it was time to move on to the meat of the faith. In their case they were what they ate, but it was time they started to eat solid food.

There are probably many people in churches today who still cling to those elementary doctrines they learned when they first believed. They haven't matured much beyond that point. It may happen for a number of reasons. One could be that they are content where they are and can't be bothered with challenge. Another might be that life's perplexities are enough to cope with, and uncertainties of faith just cannot be digested. Some may have ventured forth like Peter on his way across the water to Jesus, only to get scared midstream and find themselves sinking in the sea of doubt. Regardless of the reason, the author's admonition remains: "Let us leave the elementary doctrine of Christ and go on to maturity" (6:1).

Go on to maturity. That's easier said than done. Probably the first lesson to learn is that faith is not meant to be easy, it's meant to be challenging. When faith is too easy it becomes idolatrous. We get into comfortable beliefs, comfortable behavior, comfortable relationships. Soon our comfort becomes the conditioning factor. However, Christ's cross was not comfortable. It was to be endured in order to get done what was necessary. A challenging faith implies endurance of what may cause discomfort in order to attain greater good.

A second lesson is practice. Our author writes that "solid food is for the mature, for those who have their faculties trained by practice to distinguish good from evil" (5:14). Perhaps the saying is trite, but it fits: "No pain, no gain." Regardless of what may be our discipline, we know that to grow in it requires practice and more practice. Those who discipline themselves through practice enhance their abilities and over time develop their skills. Otherwise, their talents remain stagnant and their strength untried. It may be painful to forgive someone who wronged you, but through practice you may learn not to let others' opinions condition your behavior.

A third lesson is the author's own desire, which is for "each one of you to show the same earnestness in realizing the full assurance of hope until the end" (6:11). Hope is the Christian's abiding anchor. As

Paul writes, "We rejoice in our sufferings, knowing that suffering produces endurance, and endurance produces character, and character produces hope, and hope does not disappoint us, because God's love has been poured into our hearts through the Holy Spirit which has been given to us" (Rom. 5:3-5). Weaned on God's love, we can digest the solid food of the gospel.

Source of sustaining nurture and Giver of every good and perfect gift, we praise you for your love and abiding care. We turn to you for strength to endure the trials before us; guide us and uphold us as we pursue our tasks. Fortify us with your Holy Spirit and feed us on the wisdom of your teachings passed on through the ages. Make us bold in our convictions and forthright in action; fill us with that hope that does not disappoint us. For then we shall be fed the solid food of your love.

Hebrews 10:19-25   Third Week: Wednesday

STIR UP ONE ANOTHER
TO LOVE AND GOOD WORKS

The author of Hebrews does not just admonish the reader. There is first a description of what God does. For example, Jesus provides a new and living way to approach God's throne of grace. Jesus cleanses our hearts of evil conscience and provides the pure water with which our bodies are washed. Remember your baptism! Then hold fast to that confession of faith you made, attend worship regularly, and stir up one another to love and good works.

Wednesdays used to be a good time for midweek prayer services. Half the week was over. Some challenges had been faced; others awaited us. It was a time to reconnoiter, gather our thoughts, regroup, and prepare ourselves for what the rest of the week had in store. As a youth, I remember the service began with singing several hymns. Someone commented recently that hymns teach us to sing our faith. They may be our first lessons on what the church believes. When you think about it, most people probably sing hymns more often than they read the Bible. So hymns were an important reminder of what we believe.

Then the scriptures were read and a brief interpretation followed, frequently by an elder or deacon, occasionally by the pastor. After that, the people who were present were invited to share their concerns and joys encountered that week. There was some testimony to God's Spirit at work in the world and in people's lives, but a lot of the conversation had to do with requests for prayer, stages of life people were experiencing, problems of families seeking to live and grow together, and the need to surround specific persons with care and concern.

Prayers followed, often led by the pastor. The pastor's task was to embrace all we had just heard and lay it at God's feet. There was praise and thanksgiving for God's goodness and love; there was intercession on behalf of those both named and nameless who needed attention and care. There were supplications addressing the needs that were mentioned, followed by a silence which actually lasted for quite a while. The service concluded with a hymn and the benediction, and then came fellowship. The evening service never lasted more than an hour, and the hour was well spent. It was a time to stir up one another to love and good works.

Today, life's pace disallows such a service. People are on the run, and often the most we give one another is a cursory greeting along the way. We seldom gather for an extended period except in cases of emergency or for some momentous decision. Often, we communicate with one another with notes fixed by magnets attached to the refrigerator door. We have lost the leisurely ability to keep abreast of one another and have relinquished extended caregiving to hospitals and nursing homes.

Amid the pace and stress of modern-day living, the soul still needs time for refreshment and rest. Jesus will provide the new and living way to God's throne of grace as we pause to share with him our cares and concerns. It may only be minutes spent daily rather than an hour midweek. But it will be well worth the effort as we feel our hearts cleansed from an evil conscience.

And there is still no substitute for taking the time really to listen to what someone else is saying. We were a captive audience in the sanctuary on Wednesday evenings. But we can still enclose ourselves with others within God's embracing sanctuary and hear from others where they are on life's journey. Moments spent daily in such disciplines may be better than an hour used to be one day a week!

Almighty God, for you time is eternal and the sphere of your dominion is boundless, yet you have seen fit to send Christ into our time and space. We thank you for him, his gift of life and teachings, his sacrifice on our behalf, the forgiveness of our sins through his assurance of pardon, and the promise of your Spirit which he imparts to us. May our hearts be sprinkled clean as through him we draw near to your throne of grace. Purify our thoughts that we may more perfectly love you and more readily serve others as Christ bade us to do.

Hebrews 12:1-11   Third Week: Thursday
RUN THE RACE
WITH PERSEVERANCE

The author of Hebrews gets quite specific when it comes to discipline. The image is that of stripping off every unnecessary encumbrance in order to run the race set before us. Jesus has gone as the forerunner, himself enduring more than we'll ever be called on to experience. God is seen as the heavenly parent who disciplines us out of love and for our own good. At the moment discipline may be painful, but in time "it yields the peaceful fruit of righteousness to those who have been trained by it" (v. 11).

John Carmody, in his book *Holistic Spirituality,* has the readers think through their day. "Today is another opportunity to grow in God's love, manifest God's love, learn how God's love spreads throughout creation" (Paulist Press, 1983; p. 134). If he is worried or perplexed about something, or thinks that the day will be particularly testing, he tries to offer his worries to God and let the Spirit guide him through false fears and ambitions. His emphasis throughout the day, and what matters most, is not his will but God's. His discipline (and, in light of the scripture from Hebrews, we can say *our* discipline) is to do what he can, easily and graciously. He is not afraid to admit that today may mainly bring suffering: frustration, disappointment, things not going well. There may be those who will need his help: an act of kindness, competence, eyes that see new insights or ears to hear new truths. "Whatever, this day can be an adventure, if I will to see it as such. So come, Creator

Spirit, visit this mind that belongs to you; give me the strength of your love" (ibid.).

It is important then to embrace the day with activities that will both enhance others and sustain the self. Most of our day is spent at work within flawed and imperfect institutions, be they the family, business, school, church, or the bureaucracy. We encounter colleagues with needs similar to our own, themselves sometimes perplexed and preoccupied, at other times buoyant and relaxed. The challenge is to bring a sense of the sacraments to all that we do: to cleanse what is unwholesome, to make trying relationships whole, to forgive past and present annoyances; there are times when we can nourish, clothe, and bring hospitality to strangers, invite them to partake of the abundant blessings we ourselves enjoy; there will be occasions when we must ourselves discipline others, correct them or their errant ways, again out of our love and care for them. The day will be spent trying to do our best within very real physical and economic constraints, and it will be best to pursue it as an adventure, praying to God for strength sufficient to meet the waiting challenges.

Perseverance serves us well when daily we seek to accomplish a part of those tasks we keep putting off until another day. Good advice is to tackle first what you don't want to do and then busy yourself with what is less troublesome. A teacher once counseled me to do at least something toward accomplishing the one thing I kept postponing, and eventually it would be finished and out of the way.

At evening it is best to find time to reflect on the course of the day and before retiring give all that you have done over to God with thanksgiving and for God's blessing. At that time there is no sense in being anxious about what tomorrow may bring unless you take time to list tomorrow's priorities. It is also a good idea to keep paper and pencil beside your bed, since during the night the Spirit has a way of clarifying those vexing issues and giving precise direction on how you ought to pursue them. Day by day there will come the peaceful fruit of righteousness as we train ourselves to run the race with perseverance.

Spirit of the living Lord, fall afresh on us. Take us and mold us so that we will conform to your image. We thank you for your consoling embrace when we are troubled, your discipline when we stray. We thank you for strength daily to confront the challenges along our way. May we never cease to praise you, though the hours may slip quickly by and we are consumed with numerous tasks. Help us to pause, to reflect on your goodness, and to offer our accomplishments for your blessing and use.

Hebrews 13:1-6   Third Week: Friday

SHOW HOSPITALITY
TO STRANGERS

The author of the Letter to the Hebrews is about to conclude it. Before it ends there are some specific instructions that have to do with caring for one another. The people of God, including strangers, are sisters and brothers in Christ. As such, they need to show each other mutual respect. Also, there should not be undue concern over money or material matters. God will look after their needs. Since God is benevolent toward them, they should be benevolent toward one another.

Hospitality is easy when you know someone. We all have our cadre of friends with whom we are gracious. We entertain them and are entertained by them. Our doors are open to one another, and often they can come and go as they please. In that sense, to show hospitality is common and not difficult.

Lately, hospice centers have begun to develop. They take hospitality a step farther. They are planned for the terminally ill, who there receive the care they need night and day. Attendants are trained to minister to a specific illness, with a sense of compassion that encompasses the patients as they face death.

There are specialized centers for those with cancer and those with AIDS. Here hospitality has become quite focused; society has sought to provide shelters where the onus and dread of disease is realistically faced and medically met. Patients are cared for with all the love and attention to which they are entitled, without stigma but with hope.

Every day, adults face decisions with their aging parents. Parents don't want to be a burden on their children; they want to retain their dignity as they enter their twilight years. There are options to be considered, and family members discuss the choices with one another. Retirement homes are a possibility if the means are available. Sometimes Mom or Dad needs the care of a nursing home; which one would be best? Our children are opting to stay single longer. Some choose to live with their mate for some years without marriage. Others are having children and seeking to retain their single status.

Lately, the courts have been plagued with cases involving abused children. There are also abused parents. For them society is faced with finding alternate environments where they can recover their sense of identity and find some sense of worth.

Cities are still filled with street people, those for whom no shelter is permanent, no income is fixed, and no meal is expected. These people seek havens that offer short-term protection and comfort and spend their days hoping to receive the sustenance they need.

Prison reform is still required in many parts of the country. Space is not available to meet the existing demand. The jury is still out on whether rehabilitation or incarceration is preferable and for which crime is one to be preferred over the other.

As we walk into our sanctuaries weekly to worship, we carry with us these developments and decisions. They all have to do with the admonition to show hospitality to strangers. While there are no clearly defined answers, there is the affirmation, "The Lord is my helper, I will not be afraid" (v. 6). Fear will only harden our hearts to the Spirit's guidance, whereas confidence will give us strength to persevere toward a solution. God will neither fail us nor forsake us. Let that be our confession and hope.

God of compassion and warmth, you embrace us with your never-failing care and understanding. Your patience exceeds our capacity to comprehend, your forgiveness is as sure as Christ's sacrifice on our behalf, your guidance comes as does the dawn, and your wisdom is without equal. You hear our prayers as we make our pleas known; help us to be as hospitable to those who seek our understanding and care. Let us reach out to them with hands that may uphold them, arms that will embrace them, and acceptance that greets them as sisters and brothers in Christ.

Hebrews 13:7-16   Third Week: Saturday

OFFER GOD PRAISE

In the concluding chapter of the Letter to the Hebrews we get a vision of Christian commitment appropriate to the twenty-first century. That commitment will continue to be built on Jesus Christ, who is the same yesterday, today, and forever. It will not be confined to time and place but will occur where the squalor of life requires reclamation. There may be abuse; there will be sacrifice, the sacrifice of the fruit of our lips that acknowledge God's name. So "do not neglect to do good and to share what you have, for such sacrifices are pleasing to God" (v. 16).

When you think about it, everything we have and are is somehow a gift. Talk to those with some chronic illness, and they will point out how health is a gift. Anyone who claims to be a self-made person has lurking somewhere in the past an opportunity, call it good fortune, or a beneficent ability that provided a break. Even those who are seemingly bereft of the common necessities for decent living are still surrounded by an array of benefits. There is virtually nothing anyone can claim as rightfully his or hers alone.

The implication of that premise is that everything is likewise transient. It can be taken away as quickly as it was given. By whatever causes, a seemingly healthy person today may discover a chronic condition tomorrow. What led the so-called self-made person to success one day may lead to financial despair the next. There is hope too that conditions will change for the marginal in society and enable them to join its mainstream. No one can claim certainty in a present condition. Life is as fluid as it is fickle, and we live each day indebted to others for the gifts we are given.

This means, of course, that we should never judge ourselves superior simply because of some station we presently occupy. Rather, we should see ourselves as stewards of God's grace and benefits, recipients of that goodness that has been poured out to us. As stewards we are to care for those gifts received and see to it that they are returned to God with thanksgiving and praise and in better condition than when we received them.

Likewise our gifts should be poured out to build up others, particularly those whose squalor does not give them much hope. In that sense, the extent to which Jesus went to reclaim our lives serves as a clarion call to all who would follow him. We should not be afraid to venture among the refuge dumps of society, since he has been there already and reclaimed them as sacred ground. Today, and particularly into the next century, we are learning that even our garbage is important to God, and no thing, just as no one, can be discarded without first considering the implications for ourselves, our neighbors, the environment, and the planet.

So we are left with the author's formula for fitting behavior as stewards of God's grace: "Do not neglect to do good and to share what you have, for such sacrifices are pleasing to God." A good framework for the day's activities would be the prayer that all we do may be to God's honor and glory. That would cut short the temptation to self-service and vainglory. It would also help us to stop and think of the benefits of our actions to others. Within that framework it would likewise be well to encompass each day with thanksgiving for large and small mercies received. That would hinder undue boasting and limit selfish tendencies. Then to share our blessings with society's outcasts will be to entertain God's angels and to join with Jesus in building the city of the future, where all shall come and live with our Lord.

Source of eternal praise and thanksgiving, we offer you our sacrifice of time, talent, and earthly resources. May all that we do throughout the course of this day be to your honor and glory. Take what accords with your will and enhance its benefits; toward that which is contrary to your will, frustrate our efforts. Help us to view all of life as a sacred trust, ourselves as stewards of the benefits you bestow on us. May we reach out to those on the margins, uplift them to stand with us in exclaiming your glory, and in so doing herald the coming of the Prince of Peace.

FOURTH WEEK

John 3:16-21   December 18

LIVE IN THE LIGHT
OF GOD'S LOVE

John makes the classic affirmation that is flashed
at sporting events seen on national television, posted
on rocks and viaducts along our highways, taught
children to memorize as soon as they are capable,
and cited time and again as proof of God's love: "For
God so loved the world that he gave his only Son,
that whoever believes in him should not perish but
have eternal life" (v. 16). To live in light of that
affirmation is meant to dispel the doubt and forebod-
ing that otherwise can consume us.

How often have you spent from 2 to 4 A.M. sleepless and tossing to and fro in bed consumed with a
list of cares awaiting some resolution? Just as the first
rays of sun appear to announce that the night is soon
spent and a new day has come, you fall fast asleep—
only to be awakened by the alarm an hour later and
sleepily haul yourself out of bed to face the new day,
hardly refreshed and somewhat antagonistic for
having kept yet another vigil pondering what needs
to be done to resolve your dilemmas.

Somehow with the dawn the doubts leave us, and
the dilemmas that throughout the night were so vexing are put into perspective—or, at least, are made to
wait their turn—since more pressing matters and
routines take priority for resolution. That is, until
once again we face the night and sleep allows the
subconscious free rein, and once again those sub-
merged cares and concerns bubble to the surface. We
are faced with them for yet another sleepless turn! If
somehow we could live in the light of God's love so

that such cares could not consume us, we might pass through the night without these interruptions.

Some have found solace in reciting the Lord's Prayer and seeking to apply each strophe to their lives. "Thy kingdom come, thy will be done" has a calming effect on us. There is little sense in praying for God's will if otherwise we seek to condition every moment of our lives. To believe in God's kingdom coming in daily events is to put ourselves in the lap of God's benevolence, there to feel God's embrace and care.

"Give us this day our daily bread" is another way of putting cares in perspective. There is wisdom in caring for what can be resolved daily and commitment to doing whatever is necessary. Beyond that, those vexations still awaiting resolution are best set aside until insight and strength occur to deal with them. God does have a way of granting perspective and ability to care for our present concerns.

"Forgive us our debts, as we forgive our debtors" should be an oft-repeated plea throughout the day. Asking God's forgiveness is a way of wiping clean the slate and removing needless burdens from our shoulders. Christ assures us of forgiveness, and it is difficult at the same time not to forgive others. So, the strophe brings a two-sided benefit. Our guilt is removed, as well as our resentment, and a clean conscience is restored.

"Lead us not into temptation, but deliver us from evil" helps us to put into perspective just what we can and cannot do. Sometimes in the dark of night we are tempted to commit ourselves to ill-designed plans. Or decisions made in the throes of anxiety may overextend our abilities and be nonproductive. This particular strophe is a plea for God's guidance, the confession that we are prone to mismanage our affairs and the assurance that the Holy Spirit will accompany us.

"For thine is the kingdom and the power and the glory" puts our life in its proper perspective and returns our thoughts to where they ought to be. Put yourself at the disposal of the God who cared enough to send Christ into the world. That same God can see us through the night and into the dawn of a new day. We can rejoice in the promise of Christ's resurrection, refreshed and bathed in the light of God's love.

Our Father who art in heaven, hallowed be thy name. Thy kingdom come, thy will be done, on earth as it is in heaven. Give us this day our daily bread; and forgive us our debts, as we forgive our debtors; and lead us not into temptation, but deliver us from evil. For thine is the kingdom and the power and the glory, forever.

Luke 1:1-25   December 19

DO NOT BE AFRAID

Zechariah, confronted by an angel of the Lord, is afraid. The angel brings good news: Elizabeth, his wife, will bear a son whose name shall be John. They will receive great joy and gladness. John will be filled with the Holy Spirit, "to make ready for the Lord a people prepared" (v. 17).

Holidays can be frightening! Particularly at Christmas, people get depressed and dread the time when they may be alone. Others are celebrating the day with family and friends, but all they have are memories of happier days and they are afraid. Or there is the fear that maybe the day won't measure up to everyone's expectations. Gifts bought will not be appreciated. Tensions may surface that dampen the holiday spirit. Or the frenzy of last-minute shopping and preparation just adds increased burdens to an already overextended calendar. For a number of reasons holidays can be a frightening time of the year.

Sometimes people are afraid of God's encroachment in their lives. Scrooge thought Christmas was just so much humbug. Zechariah was startled when Gabriel appeared. There are those who don't pray as much as they ought, since they are afraid that God will answer their prayers. People order their lives in ways that produce safe and comfortable routines. Any interruption sets them in disarray, and particularly something as bold as God's intervention can have a disquieting effect.

Fear has a way of mobilizing the body's defense

mechanism so that anticipated pain will not be so discomforting. Often we hear that someone expects the worst. Anything short of that only lessens the impact. To be told that there is nothing to fear doesn't ring true in light of past circumstances when the lack of fear has left someone vulnerable and often perplexed. To be afraid in that sense is to retain some semblance of self-control and protection from a real or imaginary affliction.

Ah, but Isaiah foresees the time when God will be Israel's protection: " 'You are my servant, I have chosen you and not cast you off'; fear not, for I am with you, be not dismayed, for I am your God; I will strengthen you, I will help you, I will uphold you with my victorious right hand" (Isa. 41:9-10). Psalm 111 reminds us that dependence on God is better than self-control: God's righteousness endures forever. "The Lord is gracious and merciful. He provides food for those who fear him. . . . He has shown his people the power of his works, in giving them the heritage of the nations. The works of his hands are faithful and just; all his precepts are trustworthy. . . . The fear of the LORD is the beginning of wisdom; a good understanding have all those who practice it" (Ps. 111:10). Elsewhere the psalmist could write, "The LORD is my light and my salvation; whom shall I fear? The LORD is the stronghold of my life; of whom shall I be afraid?" (Ps. 27:1).

The testimony of scripture is trustworthy: God will deliver those who trust in the Lord. What would happen if you were to give Gabriel's gift to those about you, "Do not be afraid"? Well, for one thing, you would see to it that someone afraid of being lonely was embraced with God's love and care. Another would be that you would become a messenger of great joy and gladness. Another, that you would help those who fear their gifts might not be appreciated to know how much more valuable is the gift of love and understanding. You could teach those overextended with the frenzy of the season how to relax and absorb the goodwill that people exude at this time of year. You could tell those afraid to pray that God has once and for all answered our prayers in the gift of the Christ child. Then to those in need of self-control and protection you would become living testimony of what it means to trust in the Lord. What a gift that would be!

You have shown your people the power of your works, O God, in giving them the heritage of the nations. The works of your hands are faithful and just; all your precepts are trustworthy. Teach us to fear you so that we may be wise. You are our light and our salvation: whom shall we fear? You are the stronghold of our lives; of whom shall we be afraid?

Luke 1:26-38   December 20

RECEIVE GOD'S GREETING

Gabriel visits Mary and greets her in a troubling way. "Hail, O favored one, the Lord is with you!" Mary learns that she has found favor with God and will conceive a son whose name shall be Jesus. He will reign over the house of Jacob, and there will be no end to his kingdom. The Holy Spirit will see to the birth, since with God nothing is impossible. Mary responds that she is the handmaid of the Lord, and with that the stage is set for the birth of the Christ child.

Christmas is a time for sending and receiving greetings. Lists are found from last year, dusted off, amended, and updated; cards are bought and prepared; notes are written on some, chronicling the events of the year about over; stamps are affixed; and off they go to be mailed. Then daily, I wait for the mail to come, read the greetings from friends far and near, note the changes that have occurred in their lives, amend the mailing lists, and then display the cards for all to enjoy during the festive season. The process seldom varies from year to year. Oh, sometimes I tire of it and vow that next year things will be different; I'll only send out cards to some and not others. But then I yearn to hear from those with whom I've lost contact, and the list gets longer once again.

Christ's birth was the time for God's greeting: "Hail, O favored one, the Lord is with you!" God chose a startling way to communicate love. A child, helpless, dependent, full of promise as well as the possibility of failure, nevertheless implanted in Mary's womb, there to be nurtured at one with her and all humanity until it came time for her to give birth.

As it was with Mary, so in time it would be with all humankind: Christ within you, alive and growing, about to be born in countless acts of goodwill. "Hail, O favored one, the Lord is with you!" There would be no denying God's presence. It would be known in the life, death, and resurrection of the one whom Mary named Jesus. It would be learned in his straightforward teachings. It would be grasped in response to his call to "come, follow me," and to join with him on the pilgrimage of discipleship. It would be displayed to all the world as we, Christ's disciples, reached out to touch others in ways that reveal the Christ in each of us.

Greetings nowadays come in so many ways. Some are sincere, especially to those we care about. We ask how they are and what they've been up to, fully expecting an answer and committing some time to communicate with them. Other greetings are more superficial, especially to those we meet casually or seldom. A cursory "Hello, how are you?" is all that's exchanged as we go on about our business; nothing more is expected.

"Have a Merry Christmas and a joyous New Year" is popular now, and it, too, comes in many variations. With some we want to elaborate and append notes on news of the family; with others the simple card will suffice to let friends know we're thinking of them. In whatever fashion, greetings are a way of extending ourselves beyond the close confines of our own intimacy. Greetings break down walls of separation that may have been erected for whatever reasons. They have a way of expressing care, concern, interest in another's well-being, even curiosity—all those attributes that communicate the need we have for other people in our lives.

God expressed once and for all that same need when the angel greeted Mary. At that moment God became very human in order to express the same care, concern, and interest for even the least of God's creatures. Here was Emmanuel, God with us, implanted in Mary's womb. Henceforth, Christians would give and receive a variation of Gabriel's greeting—"The Lord be with you"; "And also with you"—for so he was and so he shall be forever!

Come, Creator, Spirit, and enter our lives; help us to be filled with your love, consumed with desire to serve you more faithfully, and driven by that quest for the truth that can set us free, Jesus Christ, the Light of the world. We give you thanks for Mary, your handmaid, and the love she bore to fruition, for Jesus, the Christ child, Emmanuel, God with us. May we likewise grow in the same wisdom and stature he taught his disciples, so that in all we do we shall give you honor and glory.

MAGNIFY THE LORD

When Mary visits Elizabeth, more occurs than just simple greetings. Elizabeth's baby leaps in her womb at the sound of Mary's voice. Elizabeth herself is filled with the Holy Spirit and exclaims how greatly Mary is blessed. Mary proclaims that her soul praises the Lord, and her spirit rejoices because of God her Savior. From now on all nations will know that God has done great things for Mary and will do great things for all people.

Some years ago for Christmas I received a telescope. It was not fancy, but it was strong enough to study the heavens. So there I'd be during the clear winter nights, all bundled up, eye to the scope, seeking to discern what planet or constellation or particular star I was studying. It was amazing how the telescope magnified those distant lights. What before was only a glimmer became a distinct object with its own uniqueness and shape. I had known them before only by name; now I could know them better, study them more easily and see them in relationship to one another. A whole new vista was magnified before me.

Mary must have felt the same way as the infant Jesus grew in her womb. She has been called by some the first Christian disciple. She believed that Jesus would bring a new vista of life to all who believed in him. He would prove to the nations how each person was unique, a distinct creation of God's loving care, with strengths and weaknesses, all of which Jesus himself could understand. He would help the people to live in relationship with one another, urge reconciliation where hatred kept persons apart, and ultimately gain for each one of us forgiveness of our sins. He would portray, as though on a huge screen, God's plan for all of creation, God's desire that wars cease and there be peace on earth, and God's commandments that we worship no other gods and show the same love for our neighbors that we heap on ourselves. Mary's soul praised the Lord as the child grew in her womb.

My wife has a mirror that magnifies. On occasion I have used it to detect the size of a blemish. I've thought to myself, Why have such mirrors? They only enlarge what you already know to be true. But, as I am told, such mirrors do help in the application of makeup, cleansing the skin, and helping to preserve the natural beauty that's there.

Think how Jesus magnifies our lives for us, showing us both our beauty and our ugly side. He puts us in perspective with ourselves: who we can become, what we have to work with, the scars, the beauty marks, the wrinkles, creases, and lines of time. He helps us to see ourselves as we really are.

Loren Eiseley, in his book *All the Strange Hours,* remembers that when his aunt died he found a beautiful silver-backed Victorian hand mirror. It had been one of a pair his maternal grandfather had given to his girls. Eiseley thought of the time when he had looked into his mother's mirror as a child, admiring the scrollwork on the silver. He could not remember when his mother's mirror vanished. It just disappeared and with it the face of a child, his own face. He goes on to write, "Nothing is lost, but it can never be again as it was. You will only find the bits and cry out because they were yourself. Nothing can begin again and go right, but still it is you, your mind, picking endlessly over the splintered glass of a mirror dropped and broken long ago" (Charles Scribner's Sons, 1975; pp. 3–4).

Jesus takes those bits and pieces of our sometimes shattered lives, puts them all together, and then holds the finished product up as a mirror for us to see ourselves anew. As Eiseley writes, we cannot go back to the beginning, but we can start anew. For what we see is what God in Christ intends for us, a whole that is healed, loved, and cared for, a creation God sent Jesus into the world to restore. Mary's soul magnified that love as she bore the Christ child in her womb.

Bathed in the splendor of your love, O God, we come with thanksgiving for your mercy and grace. You lead us through the valleys of life and lift us to the summit of your forgiveness and hope. Wherever we go, you are near; whatever we do, you know the outcome before we do. You have sent your Son to accompany us through the good and bad times. Help us to follow where he would have us go.

Luke 1:57-66   December 22

REJOICE WITH THOSE
WHO REJOICE

Elizabeth delivers her child, and all those gathered rejoice at the birth. When it comes time to name the infant she has definite plans. "He shall be called John." Zechariah confirms her choice by writing the name on a tablet. Then a strange thing happens: Zechariah's tongue is loosed, and he speaks for the first time since the angel visited him. News gets around the countryside that the hand of the Lord has had something to do with what is occurring.

God began the process when he named the creation. Since then, to name something or someone has been the highlight of the birth process. To name is to bestow uniqueness, identity, and purpose to life. With the name there is a heritage that is passed from one generation to another. The name heralds to all who have ears to hear the announcement that a new creature is among us, and may the creation be richer for the arrival.

Elizabeth's child would be called John, of that she was sure. We now know that John would become a name synonymous with Jesus' arrival. He would be the forerunner of the one who would come to heal the world and set the creation aright. John, like Jesus, was set apart by God for significant tasks within God's scheme of salvation history.

Our name similarly sets us apart for significant tasks. We are known by our name. People seek to learn our names, just as to know others' names helps us to distinguish them from one another. We have heard how some people seek to make a name for themselves. In that case they want their name to be recognizable among all others. They want their name to stand out in the crowd. We will go to great lengths for people to know us by our name and to pronounce it correctly.

Undoubtedly, you are in the process of wrapping your gifts. Think about the fact that each gift is named. There is something for Ada, Antonio, and Judith. Ellen's is set aside with her name on it and Tiffany's is next to it. When you were shopping, you undoubtedly sought just the right thing for that special person, whose name was emblazoned on your mind's eye. The final act of wrapping her or his gift will be to affix the name tag. Then you will set it apart, ready to hand to the person named and to see the delight when it is opened and shared.

The Christmas cards you've sent have all had names on them. Each name as you wrote it probably conjured an image of times past, memories of joy as well as sadness, of needs as well as strengths. The name has for a moment brought that person back into your life when perhaps you have not thought about him or her for quite some time. In that sense just your writing their names has been for you a moment of prayer, thanksgiving, intercession, or supplication for what the person has meant to you.

It was on the eighth day when John was named. Today, it would be similar to the day of our baptism. That's the day when all of us receive another name, the name Christian. Henceforth we will be known as having been set apart, marked for the rest of our lives as belonging to the household of faith. There comes with that name work to be done, much to learn as Jesus' disciples, and great joy as we are led by the Spirit. And, of course, we seek to follow the one whose name is above every name, Jesus, the Son of God.

The hand of the Lord did have something to do with what was occurring when John was born. Just as that same hand has something to do with what happens each time our name is called, we address a card, affix a name tag to that special gift, or hear a name spoken when someone is baptized. It all goes back to what God did with the creation. God named them and in so doing set them apart to God's honor and glory. That is cause for rejoicing!

All glory and honor be unto you, O God, giver of every good and perfect gift. We give you thanks for Jesus, born of Mary, Word eternal, Source of life. We give thanks for John, born of Elizabeth, your hand laid upon him, who foretold the coming of our Messiah and Lord. As you worked your wonders through these women of faith, instill your Spirit within us, that we, like them, may bear fruit worthy of your calling and give birth to generations who shall believe in your name.

REMEMBER GOD'S COVENANT

Zechariah prophesies concerning the fate of his son, John. John will go before the Lord to prepare his ways, to give knowledge of salvation to all who believe in him, and to guide the people's feet to the way of peace. That's all we hear of John until he appears, announcing that the day is at hand that all should repent and believe. In the meantime he himself has been in the wilderness, being prepared to accomplish all that his father foretold he would do.

What is your first memory of consciously being a Christian? Mine is when I was a sophomore in high school. A group of us belonged to Westminster Fellowship and gathered in the pastor's study on Tuesday mornings for Bible study and prayer. He provided the doughnuts and promised that we would have plenty of time to get to school. We provided our commitment and willingness to gather one morning a week to be led by God's word.

One morning as I was leaving, Dr. Mac put his hand on my shoulder and said that I was going to enter the ministry. That's all he said and that's all it took. From then on I was a marked person. I never questioned his decision for me or my response. I spent the rest of my formal education preparing to carry out what he foretold I would do. As I think about it now, sometimes I wonder why I responded so willingly. Then I get to pondering the fact that maybe I had nothing to do with the decision and would only have been in the way if I objected. Of course, such speculation has no answers, and today it really doesn't matter. It is just a very powerful memory of Christ's call to ministry, and I am constantly grateful that I never questioned it.

Memory is important in matters of faith. It kept God's covenant before the Israelites during their wilderness wanderings. Within Judaism it was memories of their departed loved ones that made the people aware of eternal life and wisdom passed on from age to age. As long as they remembered, the legacy would continue and lessons would never be forgotten.

Today, memories are important as families gather to celebrate the Christmas holiday. Within our family John remembers where that special ornament belongs on the tree. Jamie remembers his train from childhood and brings it out of the closet to hear its whistle once again. Eric remembers his mother's cooking and that favorite dish prepared yearly. Christmas past is remembered and with those memories persons, joys, and celebrations, are recalled and relived, adding to the festivities of the season.

As the year comes to a close, we remember the good days and the bad. For some the year has been particularly eventful; for others, routine. There are those who would just as soon forget the past and look forward with hope to a better tomorrow. Memory, however, has a way of healing past wounds. Try to forget their lessons prematurely and pain will continue to linger. Remember them, and soon they won't hurt as much as they used to. You will gain a more healing perspective.

Zechariah in his prophecy remembered God's covenant. With the coming birth of the Messiah and John's birth as a foretaste of the good news, Zechariah knew of God's deliverance and mercy. Here in two people, Jesus and John, would be living proof of

God's covenant fulfilled. What was promised to foremothers and forefathers was coming to pass. There would be a new day when all God's people would know of God's love.

During this season, we too remember God's covenant. We remember how these two women, Elizabeth and Mary, played decisive roles in God's scheme of things. Hereafter all who believed would know the extent of God's love. God came to earth in the birth of a child to comfort the lonely, heal the afflicted, care for the tormented, and raise up those who mourn. Truly, no longer can anyone say, "Know the Lord," for they shall all know the Christ, from the least of them to the greatest. Of such is the promise of God's covenant.

Blessed is our Lord and our God. You have visited and redeemed your people and caused to come forth one whom all shall call holy. He shall save your people from their sins and give knowledge of salvation to all who believe. We give thanks that we are numbered among your covenant people and pray that we may be worthy of this most costly of gifts. Let us not forget the extent of your love for us and help us work for that peace he came to proclaim.

Matthew 1:18-25 December 24

WELCOME EMMANUEL

When Mary is found to be with child of the Holy Spirit, Joseph is troubled. The angel of the Lord appears to him and keeps him from divorcing her. The child Mary is carrying is of God, come to save his people from their sins. It has taken place to fulfill the scripture: "Behold, a virgin shall conceive and bear a son, and his name shall be called Emmanuel." "God with us": what a wonderful gift! Joseph takes Mary as his wife, and when the child is born they call him Jesus.

The time had come for God to get personal. There had been the flood with its ominous presence of water surging everywhere, runaway and rampant, threatening total destruction until it receded. There had been the rainbow with its dazzling array of colors covering the whole spectrum of hues, tints, and various shadings. There had been the manna in the morning, sustenance sufficient for the day's journey as the wandering Israelites continued their trek to the promised land. When they lacked water it was found; when they needed direction there were the clouds by day and the fire by night. There had been a long succession of personnel charged with conducting the business of salvation history: judges, prophets, poets, and warriors, all of them with a vision of what it meant to be faithful to God who guided them. No doubt, God had been involved since creation began. Now God would come as one of us, as the Nicene Creed says: "God from God,

Light from Light, true God from true God, begotten, not made, of one Being with the Father."

Think of the benefits! Someone to walk with during those times of loneliness when we are in need of companionship. Someone to talk to when we are unsure of ourselves, when decisions weigh heavily upon us, or when we are anxious, even afraid. Someone to trust, who throughout history has been there whenever the people called, guiding, correcting, supporting—or reprimanding. Someone who can be counted on to provide everything necessary for each day's journey: strength, nourishment, support, health, shelter, hope, forgiveness, assurance, and confidence. That is not to say that all we have to do is sit back and wait for these benefits to come to us. Nowhere is it written that this would be the case.

Rather, there would be responsibility, the challenge to respond personally to Jesus' call to walk with him through life. Our response would get us personally involved in the whole matter of living life to its fullest, as God intended from the dawn of creation. There would be a whole new approach to all we do, a running conversation with this Jesus to see if we are behaving as he wants us to. He would no longer let us pass by anyone we see in need, for now our task would be to care for them as he cares for us.

There would be a new accountability. No longer would we answer only to ourselves and our own desires. Jesus would make perfectly clear what God intends us to be and do, in terms we could no longer confuse or misunderstand. After all, he's one of us and would show us just what it meant to be faithful: no more hiding, no more excuses, no more procrastination, no more denying or doubting God's ultimate love for us. Jesus would be there to show us the way and expect us to follow, since he would do everything necessary to assure us of abundant and unceasing life.

So our relations with other people would take on a whole new meaning. No longer would we need to put others down in order to build ourselves up. Rather, we could accept them as they are and care for them just as Christ accepts and cares for us. We could reach out to our enemies and engage them in the hard talk of reconciliation because that's what Jesus did with us on God's behalf. And we would be responsible for leaving this planet in better shape than we found it, to pass on to succeeding generations to use, enjoy, and care for.

Ultimately, God had us right where God wanted us, wholly accountable and personally involved. Jesus Christ would see to it, and the Holy Spirit would be there to guide us. So on this day long ago the stage was set for a confrontation that would comfort as well as challenge the world, Emmanuel, God with us. Welcome, Jesus; may our world be stronger now that you're here.

Giver of every good and perfect gift, we thank you for this day when the angels sang, the star shone brightly, and the heavens proclaimed the birth of your Son. We lift our voices in carols of praise to you and your love. As shepherds journeyed long ago to see this thing which had come to pass, so also now we bow before you with wonder and awe. You have entered the stage of history with the promise of peace to the nations. Hosanna in the highest! Our hearts are made glad by this gift of your love.

CHRISTMASTIDE

1 John 4:7-16   Christmas Day

ABIDE IN GOD

The topic is love. Let us love one another; for love is of God and whoever loves is of God, born of God, and knows God. No one has ever seen God; however, if we love one another, God abides in us and God's love is perfected in us. Surrounded by God's Holy Spirit we are led to love one another. Jesus Christ came to show us the way. Confess Christ as the way, the truth, and the life, and God will abide in you and you will abide in God.

John's Gospel relates the fact that "there are many dwelling-places in my Father's house" (John 14:2, NEB). Jesus was about to depart from his disciples. It was as necessary as it was certain that if he did not fulfill God's will the Spirit would not come. Jesus sought to prepare his disciples for the departure. He would, after all, go and prepare the way for them. They would join him in time and be reunited in that glorious eternal existence where days dawn with joy and darkness is no more.

"There are many dwelling-places in my Father's house." It may seem strange, writing about Jesus' departure on the day when we celebrate his arrival. Yet this passage appropriately portrays the breadth of God's encompassing love, since Jesus would become the way, the truth, and the assurance of eternal life. Jesus the way would involve his believers in an active pilgrimage. Jesus the way directs us, sets our feet to moving.

"Come, follow me." Be about your life; Christ will guide you. The beauty about such a journey is that

Jesus knows the way so well. Go out into the wilderness; he is there. Be tempted by the ways of the world; he was. Go up to the heights of the mountaintop; he did. Plummet to the depths of the valley; he walked through desolate places. Get involved in the everyday affairs of the marketplace, the daily encounters with other persons, the joys of meals shared, being ministered unto, and caring for others; he was in all that.

Jesus is the way for those actively engaged in the journey of living. John called it abiding in love. He had in mind that we should be head over heels in love with life, with each other, with the hours of each day that God sees fit to give us. We should love enough to care for one another and not let moments slip by without expressing our concern. What better day to express that love than on this Christmas Day?

Jesus said also he was the truth. By that he meant he would be the great "Aha!" of life, those moments of vision and flashes of insight that illumine our horizon. He would put everything that occurred into perspective. It would be similar to being surrounded by God's Holy Spirit and sensing the surprises of life throughout the day's normal course of events. As when Tiffany opened her present and exclaimed with glee, "It's just what I wanted!" Aha! Or sitting in worship and hearing the choir sing the Christmas portion of Handel's *Messiah.* Aha! Or sitting down to dinner with the table bountifully laden and feeling a sense of thanksgiving and intimacy for and with all of God's goodness and love. Aha! Or falling exhausted into bed, after you assembled that last toy, and sensing a reassuring comfort that you have accomplished an act of commitment and love. Aha! All these moments wash over us with the cleansing waters of our being bathed in God's love and care for us. They leave us renewed as persons and convinced that life is indeed a blessed experience.

Jesus concluded with what could be the sum of the equation. Jesus the way and Jesus the truth add up to Jesus who is life. I think he meant it as an affirmation as well as an invitation: an affirmation in the sense that there is a whole lot of living available for those who believe that there are many dwelling-places in God's house, an invitation in the sense that Jesus bade his disciples to follow him, so that where he was they would be also. John wrote, "Whoever confesses that Jesus is the Son of God, God abides in him, and he in God" (v. 15). Today, we can exclaim, "How lovely is thy dwelling place, O LORD of hosts! My soul longs, yea, faints for the courts of the LORD; my heart and flesh sing for joy to the living God" (Ps. 84:1-2). How lovely is thy dwelling place, O Lord of hosts.

We enter your courts with praise and thanksgiving, O God. Our hearts are glad on this holiest of days. You have come that we may have life, and that abundantly. You have showered us with gifts beyond measure and heaped blessings about us. We have heard the glad tidings that Jesus is born. Come, Lord Jesus, and dwell in our hearts each day. Transform us in accordance with your will for us, and make us to know your love, so that all we do and say may abide in your peace and continue in your favor.

Isaiah 61:1-11   December 26

RIGHT A WRONG

The prophet exclaims that the Lord has anointed
him to bring good tidings to the afflicted, to bind up
the brokenhearted, and to proclaim liberty to the
captives. It is the year of the Lord's favor, when
those who mourn shall be comforted, and righteousness and praise shall spring forth before all the nations. Therefore, rejoice in the Lord and be clothed
in festive garments; Christ has come to set free God's
people.

Wouldn't it feel good to correct some mistake
you've made this year? The New Year is approach-
ing: time to begin again with new hope and a clean
slate. These days between Christmas and New Year's
are good times to prepare for the new. What better
way is there to make that preparation meaningful
than to begin by righting a wrong?

To right a wrong was Jesus' primary mission. That
is why it was said of him that Jesus is our righteousness. In Middle English, another form of righteousness was rightwiseness. The implication was that
something was askew. Someone needed to make it
right. Thus Jesus came to set the creation right, to
return it to God's intended design.

To believe that in Christ is our righteousness is to
believe that through Christ we are called to set
skewed relationships right. If things are not as they
should be, it would be well for us to explore how we
might improve them. That way we could enter the
new year with a clearer conscience. At least we'd feel

we had done what we could. What's the best way to begin?

First, see the relationship as it was meant to be. That is to say, we probably have to peek around the corner to see what the relationship looked like before it got skewed. If that is not possible historically, we can always approach it theologically. What does God intend the relationship to be? There are all kinds of answers to that question in the Bible. Primarily, God wants us to reconcile our differences and to care for others as we care for ourselves.

Second, once you've discovered the relationship as it was meant to be, determine the steps you'll take to restore it. It may take a while. After all, it took time to deteriorate; restoration likewise takes time. Patience and effort are always key ingredients of reconciliation. Sometimes people would rather stay angry than commit themselves to the effort it takes to heal differences.

Third, once restoration has begun, set for yourself realistic expectations. People are unique individuals, not computers. Their responses can never be programmed. Simply because you have embarked on a ministry of reconciliation does not mean that all your efforts will meet with success. Some may be lauded; others will be scorned. It may seem at times that all your efforts are futile. Set for yourself some obtainable goals along the way by which to measure your achievement. But don't be disappointed if your attempts are rebuffed. We have not always been kind to our enemies.

Fourth, there are some situations best committed to the Holy Spirit to resolve; nothing we can do will make any difference. There is no sense in wasting more time with them or worrying yourself about them any longer. Further attempts will only be futile. Perhaps time alone will heal the differences and an occasion will present itself for reconciliation. In the meantime, any effort spent will only strengthen your resolve to do something worthwhile.

Fifth, resolve not to let the thoughtless comment slip from your lips. So often an insensitive sentence said without thinking can damage an otherwise stable relationship. James calls the tongue a fire and writes that with it we can at the same time bless God and curse our neighbors. This ought not to be so. Let our tongues bless God as we build one another up. In so doing we will enhance those relationships Jesus came to establish, reconcile, and hold inviolate to God's honor and glory.

Lover of justice, we give you thanks for sending us Jesus. He comes to bring good tidings to the afflicted, build up the brokenhearted, proclaim liberty to the captives, and the opening of the prison to those who are bound. Help us in Christ to hear the clarion call to go and do likewise. Give us the strength to see beyond our own hurts and estrangement and to catch the vision of your reconciling community. Empowered by the Spirit, may we then provide the balm of your goodness and let the healing occur.

Isaiah 40:1-11   December 27

WALK WISELY

"A voice cries, 'In the wilderness prepare the way of the LORD, make straight in the desert a highway for our God.' " The vision is of the uneven ground made straight, the mountains and hills made low, the rough places now a plain. Words of comfort are spoken, with the vision of the one who will come to shepherd the flock. The message is set in the context of wisdom that has withstood the ages: "The grass withers, the flower fades; but the word of our God will stand for ever."

Jesus Christ has arrived. He can set our feet on firm ground. The admonition is to walk wisely, since everything has occurred to smooth the rough places. After all, our time on earth is short. As we face another year we are aware of how quickly the present year has passed. Likewise the future will soon be over. So it would be well for us to enter the present resolved to walk wisely: that is to say, learn from our mistakes, make the most of our time, and be not foolish.

The prophet proclaims that warfare is ended and iniquity is pardoned. We know that in Jesus our sins are forgiven. It is well to learn from those mistakes we make. The value of mistakes lies in what we do with them. Some people wallow in them like bathing in quicksand. They can't rise above the foolish things they've done and seem to sink deeper and deeper into remorse and self-pity. Soon they are beyond any rescue efforts and would rather drown

with guilt than begin the arduous task of rehabilitation.

Others wear their mistakes well. Mistakes are like
a veneer that keeps the surface from being repeatedly marred or damaged. Once committed, people
learn their lesson, which keeps them from repeatedly
falling victim to similar circumstances. Soon wisdom
accrues that enables them to detect the telltale symp-
toms. These folk are most adept at assisting others in
similar situations and often can help others to avoid
the traps that have ensnared them.

Second, make the most of your time. Time is a
sacred trust, and each moment is a gift of God's
grace. Time is not meant to be wasted, just as none
of God's gifts should be squandered. That is not to
say at times it's best just to do nothing other than to
savor the moment. To walk wisely would be to avoid
what is more often the case: to be so preoccupied that
time passes without your awareness that it's gone.
Each moment is God's eternity at a glimpse; it contains all the grace and mercy necessary for the moment as well as the promise of God's love to come.

Third, do not be foolish. Foolishness within the
Greek mentality was well defined. Fools wore masks.
In Greek theater there were tragic and comic heroes,
each with his or her own mask. The thought behind
the masks was that persons could act out a specific
role without betraying their true identity. Today,
Jesus has come so that our true identity can flourish
without the need of a mask.

The best way to avoid foolishness is to seek
Christ's will for our lives. Since Christ knows us
better than we do ourselves, since God in Christ
knows our thoughts before we utter them, since
Christ reflects God's intention at the creation, what
better way to drop the mask than to seek Christ's
will for our lives? That's why it is appropriate at the

end of our prayers to say, "Not our will but yours, O Lord."

If at the end of the day you can thank God for all that has occurred; if you can pray for forgiveness, with the assurance that Christ sits at God's right hand and there intercedes for you; if you can thereby hand over your mistakes to God, who alone knows your secret and inmost thoughts; if you can rest with the thought that you have done your best with all the mercies God has given you that day; if you can in praying remove all the pretense you may have worn, the shame you may have earned, the foolishness you have committed—then you will have walked wisely.

"O God, thou art my God, I seek thee, my soul thirsts for thee; my flesh faints for thee, as in a dry and weary land where no water is. . . . Because thy steadfast love is better than life, my lips will praise thee. So I will bless thee as long as I live; I will lift up my hands and call on thy name. My soul is feasted as with marrow and fat, and my mouth praises thee with joyful lips, when I think of thee upon my bed, and meditate on thee in the watches of the night; for thou hast been my help, and in the shadow of thy wings I sing for joy" (Ps. 63:1, 3-8).

Psalm 139:1-6, 13-18, 23-24   December 28

BITE YOUR TONGUE

The psalmist knows he is watched over and cared for. Such knowledge is almost incomprehensible. Before words form, God knows what they'll be. Stand or sit, God watches over both. Hide, God will find you; seek, God will guide your search. There is nothing God does not know, a knowledge as vast as the endless seashore. Count the grains of sand; God's oversight and care exceed the total. God knows our hearts and thoughts and can lead us in everlasting ways.

Not long ago, I came across the "Prayer of a Realist." Its source is unknown but its words are poignant. "Lord, thou knowest I am growing older. Keep me from becoming talkative and possessed with the idea that I must express myself on every subject. Release me from the craving to straighten out everyone's affairs. Keep me from the recital of endless detail. Give me wings to get to the point. Seal my lips when I am inclined to tell of my aches and pains. They are increasing with the years, and my love to speak of them grows sweeter as time goes by. Teach me the glorious lesson that occasionally I may be wrong. Make me thoughtful but not nosy, helpful but not bossy. With my vast store of wisdom and experience, it does seem a pity not to use it all. But thou knowest, Lord, that I want a few friends at the end."

It does seem a pity to come to the end of another year and not to have used that vast store of wisdom and experience inherent in each of us. Yet we will all probably retain a few friends on into the new year because we haven't. The Lord knows how tempting it's been to convince so many how right we are about so much. Yet, again, haven't things gone smoother when we cooperated rather than commanded? As the psalmist wrote, "Search me, O God, and know my heart! Try me and know my thoughts! And see if there be any wicked way in me, and lead me in the way everlasting" (vs. 23-24).

James writes similarly when he says, "Let every man be quick to hear, slow to speak, slow to anger, for the anger of man does not work the righteousness of God" (James 1:19-20). Quick to hear and slow to speak—this is probably the reason God gave us two ears and one mouth. James goes on at length about what a weapon the tongue is. People use it to lash out at others and spread malicious stories. Some churches have persons in charge of "rumor control," just to keep the potential blaze of rampant tongues contained.

Usually those persons most prone to talk too much have a real problem hearing others. Oh, they hasten to them, but what they hear is just noise. Often what they're doing is waiting for the noise to stop so they can start talking again. They are the ones who need to pray, "Keep me from becoming talkative and possessed with the idea that I must express myself on every subject."

God gave us two ears and one mouth in order to assimilate as much as we can before we issue a judgment. However, again, people act hastily when they have an opinion. Maybe it's best to express your opinion early and then talk about it with your friends and associates. At least, then people know your position. Assimilating as much as we can keeps us from becoming judgmental. An opinion may further conversation, but becoming judgmental hinders debate. Then sides are chosen too quickly and, as the psalmist writes, the way becomes wicked. Be quick to hear, slow to speak, and, above all, slow to anger. There were undoubtedly times this past year when you wished you had not said something, or had said it differently. If only you could have bitten your tongue! Well, as the new year approaches, there may be occasions really to hear what someone is saying, to listen behind the words to their concerns, fears, insecurities, as well as their hopes and dreams. There may then be less tendency to speak quickly with words that do more harm than good, and more opportunity to work the righteousness James recommends.

Gracious God, you search us and know us. You know our comings and our goings, our strengths and weaknesses. Not a word leaves our lips before you are aware of our utterings. Help us to bridle our tongues, so that we do not accuse others unjustly. Teach us how to offer comforting words, to speak the truth in love, to hear what others say to us, and thereby offer a measure of the benevolence you bestow upon us. May we in Christ bear one another's burdens to the mutual benefit of your household of faith.

2 Samuel 7:18-29   December 29

BLESS THIS HOUSE

David pours out his soul to God in fervent prayer. Why has God brought him this far? Of what significance is the house of David that God should set it apart for divine favor? If God does as promised, David will magnify God's name forever: "Now therefore may it please thee to bless the house of thy servant, that it may continue for ever before thee; for thou, O Lord GOD, hast spoken, and with thy blessing shall the house of thy servant be blessed for ever."

Each year, about this time, my mother started cleaning the house from top to bottom. She was Scottish, and tradition called for the house to be spotless before the new year began. The brass got polished along with the silver. You could eat off the floors; they were waxed to within an inch of their being. All the beds were changed, the laundry done, the drapes dusted, the furniture arranged. Everything eventually shone as the new year approached.

It was her way, as it had been her mother's way, of crossing the threshold from one year to the next. Symbolically, she was discharging all the evil of the past year of any further investiture. She was cleansing her space for the arrival of a new day and would have it as hospitable and spotless as possible. The old was finished and gone, and the new was about to begin.

Along with her rite of passage there were, of course, all the good memories: memories of the year's significant events and their principal players;

memories of those who had graced our home with their presence and left their mark indelibly etched on our collective mind; memories of God's richest blessings bestowed daily with health, strength, nurture, protection, and sustaining care that continued to envelop us in the same way as did the security blanket I carried about the house. It was her way of passing through each room and allotting a significant amount of time to what occurred there, her way of offering to God praise and thanksgiving for the year and its blessings.

Then would come the baking. As though she didn't have enough to do or had not done enough already, the board had to be spread with a bounty sufficient for all the well-wishers who'd come calling. Within Scottish tradition, even among our transplanted Scots family, the practice continued. Beginning with the first foot over the threshold in the new year, they came, a steady stream of family and friends to sample the fare and offer their best wishes for the days ahead.

In a way, all that happened was similar to what David prayed. Bless this house. Cleanse the space of everything that mars the otherwise beautiful surroundings. The beauty of the old year ending is that there is a timely transition between what was and what is yet to be. What was can be cleansed and corrected in order to allow what is yet to be to flourish unblemished. The past is over and done, and in many respects thank God it is. A whole new future awaits us, full of promise and hope.

Part of that promise is based on memories of all the blessings we've received throughout the year. Each part of our lives, just as each room of the house, has been touched in some way by the hand of God's compassion and care. Bless the house with thanksgiving for the bounty you've received and the promise God ordains through faithfulness which has never failed us.

Hope lies within the hospitality extended to all those who continue to surround us through good times and bad. Whether close family or friends or simply associates encountered during brief visits, there is a legion of supporters who dwell with us in the household of faith. To bless the house is likewise to thank God for their abiding presence and continually extend to them the welcome to come dine with us and we with them. For as we know from the Lord's Supper, of such is the kingdom of heaven, "For thou, O Lord GOD, hast spoken, and with thy blessing shall the house of thy servant be blessed for ever."

Bless this house, O God, that all who dwell herein may be touched by your merciful hand. Hold us in the embrace of your compassionate care for us, that we may be uplifted by your Spirit and upheld by your will. Keep us from straying in ways that thwart your intentions, from overlooking past weaknesses and refusing to go where you would guide us. Make us as mindful of the past as we are hopeful for the future; thereby we offer the present to receive your blessing, that it may give you honor.

LET YOUR LIGHT SHINE

"In the beginning was the Word." How well we know that; how often we've heard it. In him was life, and the life was the light of the world. Christ has come to illuminate the horizon, to shine forth on the way we should travel, to dispel the frightening worries when we come to forks in the road, and to be the beacon that leads to safe harbor. Let Christ shine in your life so that others may see the light and glorify God.

What difference does Christ make? Our hope is that Christ makes all the difference, that in the course of a day you radiate a certain exuberance that reflects your faith. The difference at times may be clearly noticeable, at other times not recognizable at all. Yet you know it, because you stand on a sure foundation. You believe that the Spirit of Christ guides you, and you trust in the way you're led. That's not to say everything henceforth will be placid and rosy; it won't. However, even in the midst of storm-tossed turbulence, you will retain a stability that comes from God, and this will sustain you throughout the course of your day.

What difference has Christ made this past year? Has Christ led you into ventures where you otherwise might not have gone, and where you gained more trust because you obeyed? That's the way it is with faith. Faith moves us out of the comfortable grooves we make for ourselves and helps us traverse terrain previously unknown to us. Whether it be through outreach to assist others in need of our care, or new horizons of understanding previously unthought of, or new awareness that comes from trials endured and overcome, or whatever paths we've pursued, faith is what allows us to take those halting first steps toward greater obedience.

What difference will Christ make this next year? More than before. That's how we grow in faith, allowing ourselves to be used by Christ in ever-increasing ways. To be used by Christ means wanting to know his will for our lives. Such knowledge comes through prayer, meditation, and study. It comes through interaction with other people, walking together in the pilgrimage of faith. It comes through the decisions we make, how we behave toward other people, within the workplace and even at play. It comes from seeking to make the light of God's love a radiant part of all that we do.

So let your light shine. Let Christ shine in your life so that others may see the light and glorify God. For some the light may mean freedom to stand out in a crowd. They won't always need to behave like the masses, since they march to the beat of a different drummer. They will be willing to take a stand on issues that affect others' lives and well-being, even when such a stand is unpopular. They will come to the aid of people's rights even when their voices are the only ones heard. They will be courageous when others are timid and bold when weakness is prevalent. Their light may be only a beacon of hope on an otherwise obscured horizon.

For others the light may be a glimmer that refuses to be extinguished. Although the winds of adversity are howling about them and the storms of life rain mightily upon them, these people will look to their faith as their only guide to haven and rest. For them the glimmer is hope, security, a source of confidence, and the means to perseverance. It gives them hope when they hear how Christ endured persecution. There is security in the fact that Christ intercedes for them and God knows their plight. They are confident that Christ is there to guide them as they ride out the waves on the stormy seas. Their means of perseverance remains the Light of the world who throughout the years has never gone out.

Throughout the new year there may be times when you stand tall with your feet firmly planted, a beacon of light that can guide others home. There may be times when your life itself is reduced to a flicker due to circumstances you do not now foresee. Through it all let your light shine, for you can rest assured that the light will be the light of Christ, who "became flesh and dwelt among us, full of grace and truth."

Light of the world, we give you thanks that you are there to guide us. You are the beacon of our faith. When we are far offshore, tossed about by the waves of turbulent seas, you guide us to safety. You steer us through the shoals of our own making, the rough places that harm us, and give us direction when we seem aimless and lost. Shine forth in our lives, that we may radiate your direction and thereby lead others to know you as the pilot of their lives.

1 Thessalonians 5:12-24   December 31

GIVE THANKS
IN ALL CIRCUMSTANCES

Paul concludes his First Letter to the Thessalonian church with some sound advice: Be at peace among yourselves and respect your leaders. Encourage the weak and admonish the idlers. Above all do not repay evil for evil, but seek to do good to one another. Rejoice always, pray constantly, and give thanks in all circumstances, for that is God's will. God will sanctify you and keep you blameless, since the God who calls you is faithful.

That is to say, wipe clean the slate! The old year is past and we stand on the threshold of a new opportunity—an opportunity to be more faithful to Christ in all that we do. Through God's mercy and grace, forgive those who have wronged you. It only frustrates God's desire for reconciliation and peace when you hold grudges. Christ has already come to repair the damage and set skewed relationships right, so drop the feelings of animosity and strife and let healing occur.

Do not condone idleness and inactivity; the kingdom is far too busy to afford such laziness. If there are those who need support, give it to them. Stand beside them and encourage them to greater effort, laud their accomplishments, and correct their errors. Admonish the reticent and guide them to greater effort, without malice but tactfully. As Paul writes, "Be patient with them all."

Then Paul gets to the threefold prescription applicable to everyone, a prescription that will guide us all into the new year and one that bodes well for greater faithfulness: "Rejoice always, pray constantly, give thanks in all circumstances." To rejoice always does not mean to hold on to some pie-in-the-sky by and by kind of theology. It is rather to make a realistic appraisal of where we stand in God's scheme of things. God endows each of us with gifts. Each day brings moments of strength to perform chores that will enhance God's created order. We have been given life in Christ. We have been cleansed of past sins and granted a new beginning because of Christ's sacrifice on our behalf. Even when we are overburdened with societal pressures and stress undermines our patience and resilience, we are given direction daily to put one step in front of another. To rejoice always is to walk in faith that Christ's Spirit accompanies us and empowers us in all that we do.

To pray constantly is basically to offer to God all that we think and do. There should really be nothing outside of God's oversight, correction, and guidance. In that sense prayer is an enveloping experience that accompanies us throughout all the day's endeavors. From the moment we awaken until our lids close at night all that we do is handed over to God to enhance or inhibit. That is why we can pray for God to sustain those of our efforts that accord with Christ's will and to frustrate those efforts that do not. Even in sleep our prayer is for peace and refreshment when we awake to the dawn of a new day, again to serve Christ in the assurance of resurrection to new life.

To give thanks in all circumstances is the most fragrant of offerings we can place before God's throne. There is truth to the ancient wisdom that taught our foremothers and forefathers to see the good in all things. Through whatever adversity they experienced they were upheld by the hope of a better tomorrow. That wisdom has sustained many persons through troubling times and has led them to recognize God's benevolent hand even in the throes of persecution and pain. To give thanks in all circumstances is to put ourselves at God's mercy and rest assured that in all things God will provide us with sufficient strength.

The year concludes with some sound advice on how to view the past and enter the future: "Hold fast what is good, abstain from every form of evil." That is to say, offer to God all the year's accomplishments with thanksgiving for whatever benefits they may bring. Discard whatever was evil, with thanksgiving to Christ that you are freed from its burden. Then through the guidance of the Holy Spirit look to the future with conviction and commitment to be more faithful to Christ in all that you do.

You have taught us, O God, that there is a time for everything. We give you thanks for this past year. You have upheld us during the difficult times and rejoiced with us during the good. We thank you for your abiding presence throughout our trials and tribulations, for your forgiveness of sins, for hearing our prayers both spoken and silent, for your comforting Spirit who leads us toward greater faithfulness. Guide us now over the threshold of the new year and into days of increased commitment to Christ and his will for our lives.

DRESS WELL

Paul gives some good advice about what to wear in the new year. Put on compassion, kindness, lowliness, meekness, and patience. Above all, put on love, which blends the whole wardrobe together. What dwells within you is as important as what is worn without. "Let the peace of Christ rule in your hearts" and the word of Christ enrich your day. Garbed in such fashion, you will praise God's name in all that you do.

People like to begin afresh. They look forward to a new day, resolved to make a difference and correct yesterday's errors. They anticipate the new year for the same reason. Things will be different this time, and what didn't get done last year will be tried again with more conviction and effort.

One of the more common resolutions people make is how they relate to others. In that sense Paul's writing today makes good sense. In interpersonal relationships it makes sense to show compassion, practice kindness, approach other people in lowliness and meekness, and, above all, to be patient. The Gospel message tells us that we are to love our neighbors as ourselves. All these characteristics describe well those basic ingredients that constitute love.

For example, show compassion. Compassion is that ability we develop to feel what another is experiencing. Compassion is our inoffensive and non-threatening entrance into other people's space, to sit with them there, hold their hand, talk with them, pray for them, and otherwise let them know how much we care for them.

Practice kindness. Kindness flows naturally from compassion and communicates to others that they are important to us. Kindness conditions what we do for them and generates care that will address their specific needs and help them to resolve their particular situations. Kindness in that case is oriented toward other people rather than ourselves and continues to flow until their needs are met.

To show compassion and to practice kindness naturally mean that we will approach other people in lowliness and meekness. Lowliness is that wonderful ability some people have to make their neighbors feel important. I have been in situations where in the midst of twenty or so guests the hostess made me feel the most important person at her party. Of course, her secret was that she did the same with all the others as well.

The scriptures abound with words about meekness as a trait that Christians should foster. Meekness helps others to feel that they're welcome whenever they come calling on us. The meek are hospitable people and are willing to take the time to listen to someone's story. If the story is joyous they will genuinely be glad; if it is sorrowful they will seek to comfort; if it requires some help they will pitch in to assist. The meek have that ability to put their neighbor's needs ahead of their own.

Of course, all of this requires a great deal of patience. Patience, like endurance, is one of those acquired traits that only come with experience. Those who exercise know that the longer they go the more they'll be able to do the next time. If they consistently run an extra half mile each week, soon three miles will require no extra effort. Likewise with patience: the more we practice, the greater patience we'll have. And in some cases, to wear the wardrobe Paul prescribes will take all the patience we can muster.

Yet, in so doing, at the end of the day the peace of Christ will dwell in our hearts. Our prayer will be that in word and deed all we do may be done in Christ's name, with thanksgiving to God. Clothed in such godly splendor, our thoughts will be continually inspired by Christ's word. We will need to stay attuned to that word, and this will require prayer, study, and continuing discipline. That should come as no surprise, however, since all of us know that resolutions take effort. In this case our efforts will assure that this year we're well dressed.

Gracious God, we greet the dawn of a new day with thanksgiving for Christ's promise of life everlasting. We look forward to the new year bathed afresh in your grace and mercy. We are sustained by your forgiveness of past sins, nourished on your eternal Word, and strengthened with the bread you give us each day. Help us to enter this year resolved to lead more committed and disciplined lives in response to your graciousness and more faithfully to follow the Christ in whose name we pray.

FIND YOUR NICHE

Paul begs his readers to lead a life worthy of the role to which they have been called. Some are called to be prophets, some evangelists, some pastors and teachers. The goal is a unity of faith, maturity, and the measure of the stature of the fullness of Christ. There is one body and one Spirit, one hope to which all are called, one baptism, and one God who is above all and through all and in all. The body is joined together in Christ, so find the function you're to perform for the growth and well-being of the whole.

All the world's a stage, and each one of us is called to play a part throughout the course of our lives. Shakespeare was wise when he wrote that; so also was Paul in his Letter to the Ephesians. Both of them knew the value of having a job to do, and of doing it well, and knew how the system worked with co-operation among all the parts.

Not everyone has the same talents or strengths. Some are thinkers. They envision what should be done but cannot be bothered with the work it takes to accomplish it. They are usually way ahead of other people and feel most comfortable discussing issues, philosophical arguments, theoretical options, and equations of one sort or another. We rely on these people to chart the course we'll eventually take. They are important to the system's moving ahead.

Others are doers. They are most comfortable when told what to do and don't want to be bothered with theory or speculation. They are the workers within the community; some call them the backbone of the community. They are often most content doing the tedious tasks that others don't want to do. You can rely on these people to get the work done once they're told what the work is.

A third group are the translators. They are the people who take the thinkers' visions and translate them into performable tasks for the doers to accomplish. They are important, since they have the capacity to stand with a foot in each camp. Sometimes they feel more at home with the thinkers; other times they want to be with the doers. Regardless, they go back and forth and constantly help each person to see what can be done. Paul knew well that everyone has unique gifts suitable to performing specific tasks. He stressed the importance of everyone working together. Nowhere was it said that one person is better than another, since what some would consider menial, others would see as crucial to the body's performance.

The task is to find your niche. Some congregations have "niche finders" in their midst. Their task is to get new members involved as soon as they join the church. The theory is that everyone has a job to do, and the sooner a person is involved the better. Some in the congregation are mission-oriented. They want the church involved outside its walls and find the most meaning when the congregation is committed to social activity. Others in the congregation care for the house and grounds. They are more comfortable with its internal functioning and are prone to support local causes. Both groups are necessary and natural within congregations. It's important to feel comfortable with your niche and find that your functions are appreciated.

Problems occur when we feel that people don't appreciate what we do. Factions arise when some group feels itself superior or more important than another and judges another group as less faithful than itself. Paul sought to minimize these factions and keep them from forming. That's why he stressed the importance of the church as the body of Christ. Whenever some part of the body suffered for whatever reason, it would affect the whole. Everyone was crucial to Christ, and the Spirit depended on the cohesion that resulted from coordinated efforts. No one can do everything, nor should anyone try. The closest we get to it are the translators, those who understand people's unique gifts and get everyone working together. All the world *is* a stage, and each one of us will have a part to play. Find your role and work well with others as all of us seek to attain maturity in Christ.

O God, we give you thanks that in Christ you call us and set us apart. You name us and endow us with gifts and talents, thanks to your grace. Help us to fit within Christ's household and find our place within your scheme for the creation. Outfit us for the tasks you have in store for us and blend our efforts with those of our co-workers. Keep us from entangling your intentions with our own need for recognition and from subverting your will by letting ours get in the way. May we be faithful to Christ, who calls us, and obey the commandments he clearly sets forth.

Ephesians 4:17-32   January 3

RELIEVE YOUR TENSION

Paul advises his readers to put off their old nature, hardness of heart, callousness, ignorance, greed, and licentiousness. They are to put on the new nature, "created after the likeness of God in true righteousness and holiness." Clothed in such garb they will speak the truth with their neighbors, will not let the sun set on their anger, will do honest labor, and will otherwise be kind to one another. To follow his advice could help all of us to relieve some of our tension.

Often, it's very difficult to speak the truth with your neighbor, especially when the truth hurts. However, it hurts worse when criticism is told to everyone except the one to whom it's directed. The better course of action is to express your concerns honestly, openly, and gently with those who are responsible. That would allow healing to happen rather than letting the sore continue to fester.

Paul wrote that "we are members one of another" (v. 25). Elsewhere he said, "If one member suffers, all suffer together" (1 Cor. 12:26). Let us take that affirmation seriously and remember that if one part of the body hurts, it will affect the whole. The eye cannot function well when the thumb is broken, nor the ear hear so well when the mouth is sore.

The Lord's Table is a classic reminder that we are members one of another. We can heartily disagree, we can be angry, we can rejoice and dance together, we can grieve for one another. At the end of the day we will all join together around Christ's Table.

Christ extends the invitation to all. They will come from east and west, north and south, and sit at the Table regardless of status, race, sex, or mental or physical disabilities and be nurtured by the sustenance of Christ's body broken and given for them. The Lord's Table remains the classic reminder to us to speak the truth with one another.

Second, Paul reminds us to "be angry, but do not sin." Anger shows that people care enough to be honest with one another. Too many people think Christians should never get angry. They have the notion that they should always be sweet with one another. The church, however, is the best place for its people to vent their frustration and anger, if they remember at the end of the day to say "The peace of Christ be with you" and go to the Lord's Table together.

For those who would rather stay angry than do the hard work of reconciliation, Paul writes, "Do not let the sun go down on your anger." Each day that the sun sets without some sort of resolution, whatever initially caused the anger gets blown further and further out of proportion. Soon, the anger itself becomes distorted to the point of divisiveness, while its original cause is all but forgotten. If the truth provokes anger so be it, but work toward reconciliation.

Third, do honest labor. Don't expect to get something for nothing. Paul wrote that if the thief were to work then he or she could give to those in need. Again, his emphasis was upon the other person and that person's well-being rather than just on the self. Honest labor requires that we set realistic goals for ourselves. We may have to cut back in order to achieve what we can honestly attain. That's just good stewardship. Greed, on the other hand, always keeps us seeking to attain the impossible. Its pursuit keeps us self-centered and uncaring about our neighbor's needs. Paul wanted us to be caring and concerned for the neighbor.

His final bit of advice for today is to "be kind to one another, tenderhearted, forgiving one another, as God in Christ forgave you." It is amazing how prayer daily for others can break down barriers that separate us, barriers that weigh heavily upon us, anxieties and fears that continue to haunt us. Prayer daily is one of the best methods we have for staying in touch with one another and on top of what we ought to be doing in response to God's will. Along with Paul's other advice, prayer daily will help us to yield our tension to God.

Gracious God, you accompany us through all of life's ventures. You know our needs before we voice them. Through Christ you dwell in our midst, and by your Spirit you guide us with wise counsel. Help us to hear your word proclaimed through the apostles and prophets. May we sing your praises as the poets have done throughout the ages. Lift from us those burdens too heavy to carry and give us the strength to correct all our wrongdoings. Make us more reconciling in our relationships and as caring as Jesus taught us to be. For we pray in the name of him who calls us to faithfulness.

Joshua 3:14–4:7   January 4

STAND ON THE STONES

Joshua describes how Israel crossed the Jordan opposite Jericho. The priests went first, carrying the
Ark of the Covenant. As they entered the water, the
river receded and the people passed over on dry
ground. The Lord told Joshua to appoint twelve men
from the people, one from each tribe, to take twelve
stones from the middle of the Jordan. These stones
would serve as a memorial, that when Israel crossed
the river the Lord cut off the waters so the Ark of the
Covenant could precede the people as they passed
over the river on dry ground.

God remains faithful in so many ways. In spite of
the year that has just passed, the hardships and
heartaches you've endured, think of the ways that
God gave you what God promised to do. These kept
promises become the reminders of God's faithfulness, the stones that provide the foundation upon
which our faith is built, the high ground that helps
us pass through those troubling times.

First, there's the stone of relationships. Each of us
has our significant others, be they family or friends.
They are those for whom no lengthy explanations
are necessary, with whom we feel most comfortable
regardless of our moods, and to whom we entrust
our most secret fears and desires. Time is irrelevant
with such relationships; they age over the years like
fine wine. Even when we're apart for some time, it
seems as though the conversation takes up where the
last paragraph ended. We cherish those relationships
and should continue to guard them as fine treasures;

they will serve as a stone to help us over troubled times.

A second stone is the church and its ritual. Regardless of how we may feel about organized religion and how at times the bureaucracy seems to hinder the gospel, the church and its ritual has stood us well through good times and bad. Recently I have discovered again how important it is to recite daily the Lord's Prayer. It puts the day in perspective and gives it a framework surrounded by God's continuing grace and mercy. The Apostles' Creed, the Doxology, and the Gloria Patri enhance each Sunday's liturgy with timeless truths and ritual repetition without which I somehow feel that I have not worshiped. Those words provide a stability of assurance that God throughout the ages remains faithful and sure.

A third stone is our daily schedule. It's amazing how important routine is to us. It provides a semblance of security when we have things to do, projects to complete, people to meet, and goals to achieve. The daily schedule is our way of staying in touch with who we are during the passage of time and of seeing the mark we make in the course of our own history. When that routine is interrupted or for a time forsaken, we feel out of sorts and ill at ease. We should have our routine and make each day as meaningful as possible. As time passes, the accumulation of our accomplishments makes for meaningful memories.

Hobbies are an important stone. What do you like most to do when you don't have to do what you're supposed to do? Hobbies are a true mark of our character; they help us to re-create ourselves. They serve as a buffer against the demands on our time and allow us to express ourselves in distinctive ways. The question often asked by people in personnel is,

What do you do during your free time? A hobby is like a trove to be treasured, brought out from time to time and explored until its adventure and serenity lift you to the heights of serenity and satisfaction. It, too, is a stone that can help you pass over troubled waters.

A fifth stone to retain is that of service on behalf of others. There are so many things we can do. Someone has said that our prayers do not end with amen, they end with what we do in response to what we prayed. Service is an extension of our intercession, the means by which we put our words into action. Service takes seriously Jesus' admonition to provide for the needs of the hungry and the thirsty, to house the stranger, clothe the naked, care for the sick, visit the imprisoned, and otherwise care for our neighbors as God in Christ cares for the world. With service we add one more stone to the memorial to God's faithfulness.

Make of our faith a sure foundation, O God, built to withstand the troubling times and upon which we can dance during times of great joy. We thank you for Christ, the cornerstone, and for Peter, the rock upon whom the church was built. Help us to join the legions who have gone before us, the Israelites whose tribes set aside stones from the Jordan, the prophets, priests, and poets who transmitted your will, and our foremothers and forefathers who built the structures of our faith upon which we now rest. May we continue their legacy so that those who follow will house their faith upon the same sure foundation.

PAY YOUR DUES

Jonah finds himself in the belly of the fish. He calls to God out of the depths of his distress. As though he were in hell itself he feels cast out from God's presence. The waves wash over him, the waters close in about him, the bars of the pit seem to close him in forever. Then he remembers the Lord and lifts his prayers to God. With a voice of thanksgiving he makes his sacrifice and pays his vows: "Deliverance belongs to the LORD!"

Pay your dues. How often we hear someone say that. Sometimes it means that we have to earn whatever merit we receive; other times it means to gain experience. The implication is usually that we have to give something in order to get anything in return.

There's no way we could ever pay our dues before God. To begin with, God's gifts are freely given. Then there is nothing we could ever do to earn God's favor. Supposing we could pay our dues, how much would be enough? What is your life worth, and how much does your forgiveness cost? We know what it did cost, and only God could pay it. That is why it took Christ, God incarnate, to pay the ultimate price. Nothing else in all of creation could satisfy God.

So when it comes to God, what does it mean to pay your dues? Well, we already know we have not earned what we've received, so it can't mean that. It may mean to gain experience, but toward what end? There are some things we can give God, not in order to get anything in return but, rather, in response to all that God has already given us. Jonah offered the sacrifice of thanksgiving and paid God the ultimate vow, "Deliverance belongs to the LORD!"

There *are* some dues we can pay God in response to all that God has done for us. First, God is due our thanksgiving. Even when our lives seem awash with turbulence, God can be counted on to chart calm seas for us. We can turn to God with thanksgiving for each day God grants us, for the strength we gain from the Spirit, and for the assurance we have in Christ of life unending. Wherever we turn and whatever we do, God is there, as God has been throughout history, to guide our course.

Second, God is due our obedience. From the days of Abraham, God has consistently set forth clear commands. They are not a set of limitations upon our freedom, they are guides to God's will so that our lives may be full and worthy of praise. As Jonah confessed, "Those who pay regard to vain idols forsake their true loyalty." Our loyalty is to God alone, who created us and, through Christ, redeemed us from the depths of our own vainglorious hell. Only as we obey God can we live the life we were created to live, and that, indeed, is abundant.

Third, God is due our respect. It is one thing to obey someone, it is another to respect those you obey. God does not want marionettes, string puppets going through rote actions whenever God pulls the cord. God wants us to endeavor to understand what we are to do and then to appreciate God's efforts on our behalf. God wants us to seek the guidance which those of faith have passed on through the ages and then to grow into maturity day by day.

Fourth, God is due our trust. When things go well it is easy to confess that God is good. It is during stressful times that we begin to doubt God's sincerity and concern for our condition. At times we blame God as though God were whimsical with our fate.

We can trust God to grieve at our sorrow, to hurt with our pain, to feel isolated during our loneliness, and to fret when we are troubled.

Fifth, God is due our commitment, commitment in the sense that when all else is said and done we will follow God to the ends of the earth. Commitment in that sense is the culmination of thanksgiving, obedience, respect, and trust. Jonah forsook vain idols and confessed that deliverance belongs to the Lord. He was committed to worship no other lords but God alone. Such commitment will likewise rescue us from the pit and lift our eyes to the glory that awaits those who give God obedience and love.

We dwell amid the folds of your mercy, O God. Your grace encompasses all that we do. Where would we be apart from your love which sustains us? Through Christ you lift us out of our sin. We thank you for gifts you continually bestow on us, for the wisdom we gain from your holy writ. May we be led by the Word made flesh among us as we look to the Spirit for guidance and care. Make us more faithful in all our endeavors and be pleased with our efforts. In Christ's name we pray.

EPIPHANY

John 2:1-11   Epiphany

REMEMBER YOUR BAPTISM

Jesus is found at the marriage at Cana. All the
guests are assembled and the wine gives out. Jesus'
mother implores him to do something about it. Jesus
manifests his glory by turning the water to wine. The
steward, not knowing what has occurred, chides the
bridegroom for saving the good wine until after
the guests have had their fill. The servants know
what has happened and the disciples believe. In all,
the party can be counted successful.

What better way to conclude a series of meditations on Advent and the Christmas season than to
remember your baptism. It is your initiation into the
household of Christ, your invitation to come to the
party and partake of Christ's glory.

That glory will henceforth become evident in so
many ways. Just like the water at the marriage feast,
common, ordinary facts of life will be transformed
into incredible wonders not otherwise thought possible. Like the request made by Jesus' mother, a simple reality will be enough to set the Spirit working,
and the outcome will be an enhancement of God's
kingdom in your life.

Think of how your life is surrounded by fellow
members of the household, sisters and brothers of
faith. They are there to guide you and learn from
you. They seek to assist you as they depend upon
you. They enter into a covenant with you and depend upon that bond that binds you together, your
common baptism. In that sense, there is no slave or
free, male or female, black or white, for we are all

joined together in a symphony of parts playing together in God's honor and glory.

As you remember your baptism, celebrate the day
in some significant way. Think of it as your birthday,
the day you were born anew. Do something nice for
yourself, a special meal or a gift of some kind, or an
event you particularly like doing. Set aside some
time to be with a special person to celebrate the day.
Make it a memorable, extraordinary day for yourself.

Then make the day memorable for someone else,
particularly someone who might be surprised to hear
from you. The wine steward was surprised when the
good wine appeared. Be good wine for someone. It
may take a phone call or a letter or even a visit. Let
someone know you are thinking of them in a particular way that enfolds them with care on this special
day.

Make a covenant with Christ that you will be
more faithful in some particular and meaningful
way. The whole purpose of these meditations has
been to challenge us daily to be more intentional
about our faith commitment. What better way to
continue their effects on us than to launch our lives
upon an endeavor that will stretch our commitment?
Study or service of some kind is excellent, as is the
vow to continue some form of meditation.

Keep in touch with yourself. Watch for signs that
you are slipping back into routines that allow time
to pass without your being aware. Keep to a schedule
that makes moments meaningful, and remember to
dedicate each day to God's glory and honor. Don't
let your neighbors go unnoticed through your own
busyness, but keep in touch with them and their
needs.

Set for yourself a day in the future when you will
give yourself a performance review. Ash Wednesday

might be such a day, as you embark on Lent and its disciplines. Aim at that day as a time when you will look back at yourself and your faith commitment, a time to reflect on how far you've come with the decisions you've made and the growth that's occurred in the meantime. That day will also serve as a goal for some changes you want to make in your life-style.

In all that you do, celebrate your faith. Jesus came to bring us life and to enlighten our way. Remember that we live surrounded by God's Spirit and are held continuously within God's loving embrace. We shall be led as we seek to be faithful, and there shall be wonderful surprises!

Gracious God, through Christ we give thanks for new life. We remember our baptism and rejoice in the refreshing waters that washed away our sins, thanks to your grace. We rise each day to the promise of resurrection and seek to be faithful. Fill us anew with your Holy Spirit, that we may grow in the wisdom and the stature of the one who calls us to discipleship, even Christ our Lord.

INDEX OF SCRIPTURE
READINGS